LIGHTING
<u>THE</u> FIRES <u>OF</u>
FREEDOM

LIGHTING THE FIRES OF FREEDOM

African American Women in the
Civil Rights Movement

JANET DEWART BELL

THE NEW PRESS

NEW YORK
LONDON

Requests for permission to reproduce selections from this book should be mailed to: Permissions Department, The New Press, 120 Wall Street, 31st floor, New York, NY 10005.

Published in the United States by The New Press, New York, 2018
Distributed by Two Rivers Distribution

ISBN 978-1-62097-335-6 (hc)
ISBN 978-1-62097-336-3 (e-book)
CIP data is available

The New Press publishes books that promote and enrich public discussion and understanding of the issues vital to our democracy and to a more equitable world. These books are made possible by the enthusiasm of our readers; the support of a committed group of donors, large and small; the collaboration of our many partners in the independent media and the not-for-profit sector; booksellers, who often hand-sell New Press books; librarians; and above all by our authors.

www.thenewpress.com

Book design and composition by Bookbright Media
This book was set in Scala, Berkeley, and Lato

Printed in the United States of America

10 9 8 7 6 5 4 3 2 1

In memory of
Derrick Bell,
beloved husband, courageous prophet, impassioned feminist,
steadfast and gentle warrior for racial and social justice,
and
Willie Mae Neal,
beloved mother, wonder woman, freedom torch bearer, true
believer in the promise of America.

May their lives continue to inspire and guide us.

CONTENTS

LIGHTING
THE FIRES OF
FREEDOM

INTRODUCTION

The Civil Rights Movement was one of the most dramatic periods of American history, marked by rapid and profound change. During this short span of time—from the 1950s to the 1970s—African Americans led the fight to free this country from the vestiges of slavery and Jim Crow. African American women played significant roles at all levels of the Civil Rights Movement, yet too often they remain invisible to the larger public. While some African American women led causes and organizations, such as Dorothy Height, the president of Delta Sigma Theta sorority and the National Council of Negro Women, and Dovie Hudson, the NAACP president in Leake County, Mississippi, others did not have titles or official roles. Cooks such as Georgia Gilmore organized to raise money to support the Montgomery bus boycott. They didn't stand on ceremony; they simply did the work that needed to be done. They raised money and provided housing and solace—all without expectation of personal gain. These often unnamed women helped to construct the cultural architecture for change.

African American women led a wide range of efforts to desegregate public accommodations and to secure voting rights; they engaged in actions across a range of fields, including law, education, and journalism. Women leaders, such as the crusading anti-lynching journalist Ida B. Wells-Barnett and Rosa Parks, whose courageous refusal to surrender her seat to a white person sparked the Montgomery bus boycott, were also anti-rape activists, trying to protect black women from the white southern tradition of "droit de seigneur," literally, the "right of the lord." In the antebellum and Jim Crow South that meant black women's lives and bodies did not matter; white men abused and raped black women at will and without punishment. African American women leaders addressed the most important and volatile issues of the times, from segregation to lynching, from education to economic justice. Every civil rights campaign included African American women who made important intellectual and political contributions.

Prior to the Civil Rights Movement in the United States in the mid–twentieth century, African American women played significant roles in struggles for racial justice. Through activities in churches, schools, organizations, and the black women's club movement, African American women were integral to their communities' survival and advancement—developing social justice and social programs. In particular, the black women's club movement, which started in the late nineteenth century through a concerted effort to combat lynching, developed organizational and leadership skills. The National Association of Colored Women's Clubs, founded in 1896, had the motto "lifting as we climb," meaning that as African American women worked to climb the social and economic ladders, they intentionally and simultaneously lifted African American communities. This tradition of service and sacrifice laid an aspirational and practical foundation for women's leadership during the Civil Rights Movement, by recognizing social responsibility and community organizing.

There were many civil rights leaders throughout the country. People put their lives on the line through direct action, such as sit-ins, freedom rides, and legal challenges including the children and parents of those first to integrate schools and other public facilities; they were dramatic catalysts for transformative change. People who lived and worked in the heat of the civil rights cauldron were without question the heart and soul of the Movement. Their heroic actions—often putting themselves and their families in harm's way—were without equal. Myrlie Evers always knew the dangers that she and her husband faced, but they persisted. The young people of SNCC, exemplified by Judy Richardson, worked in hostile environments and faced

direct assaults. People who raised funds or provided housing and
food to civil rights workers put their own lives and livelihoods in
jeopardy. In many instances, isolated and vulnerable sharecropper
families in the rural South participated in the Civil Rights Movement in this way. Leah Chase, in defiance of Jim Crow laws, provided more than food to civil rights workers; she provided a safe
haven. Some other participants' contributions were not as dramatic
or fraught with danger but necessary to the freedom struggle. June
Jackson Christmas and her husband, Walter, opened their home in
New York City to provide respite for civil rights workers from the
South. She also provided counseling and fundraising support.

Beyond Rosa Parks, Coretta Scott King, and Dorothy Height,
most Americans would find it difficult to name women civil rights
leaders—though there were many. *Lighting the Fires of Freedom*
presents interviews with nine women leaders in the Civil Rights
Movement, some well-known and some not. Leah Chase, June Jackson Christmas, Aileen Hernandez, Diane Nash, Judy Richardson,
Kathleen Cleaver, Gay McDougall, Gloria Richardson, and Myrlie
Evers all have wonderful and complex stories. Their stories are in
the tradition of earlier women engaged in freedom struggles such
as Mary McLeod Bethune, Ida B. Wells-Barnett, and Nannie Helen
Burroughs. Like these earlier heroines, the individual and collective
life journeys of the women in this book provide inspiration and lessons upon which today's social movements can build. In their passionate and committed lives, these women confronted American
racism with bold resolve.

African American Women as Leaders

Black women brought unique focus and perspectives to their
work as leaders in the Civil Rights Movement. With double
consciousness—awareness of sex and race—and triple consciousness adding class, these women did work that was a pragmatic and

necessary response to societal conditions. In *Fighting Words: Black Women and the Search for Justice*, Patricia Hill Collins describes Sojourner Truth's "tradition of visionary pragmatism . . . informed by race, class and gender intersectionality, as well as pragmatic actions taken in search of freedom" (p. 240). Collins's description of Truth illuminates the tradition of African American women's leadership. Black women's leadership often embodies three modes: transformational leadership, servant leadership, and adaptive leadership.

To achieve transformative change, African American women had to be creative and adapt nontraditional approaches for their particular circumstances. Eschewing top-down leadership, they encouraged people to develop their own approaches, then supported them to achieve their goals. This practice defines transformational leadership. For example, Diane Nash's "diligence," her insistence on reliability and consistency, helped develop an environment of trust so that people could focus on solutions as well as logistical details. Judy Richardson understood the vital significance of running the SNCC telephone service—literally a lifeline for civil rights workers. She listened to what activists needed and provided the service.

Respect is an important value of transformational leadership. Respect manifests in many forms, including being reliable, showing up when needed, being transparent about intentions and process, and being inclusive. Enacting this value, Nash and Richardson motivated and inspired others. Transformational leadership changes social systems as well as individuals. It encourages maximum participation and the taking on of leadership roles to effect positive change.

Servant leaders are rooted in their desire first to serve their communities as opposed to gaining power for themselves. African American women embraced work without recognition, but they also realized that strategic recognition helped to foster the work. Servant does not mean servile. The ultimate servant leader was Jesus, and African American women have used this model of leadership for generations. Harriet Tubman was a remarkable servant leader. As a "conductor" on the Underground Railroad, she led hundreds of slaves to freedom and also worked as a Union scout and spy. After the Civil War, she moved to upstate New York and established a home for the aged. She never sought personal gain and continued to sacrifice to help others. She was generous and humble, defining traits of African American women social justice leaders.

Adaptive leadership ensures that leaders thrive in challenging environments and receive the support and sustenance necessary to continue their leadership work over a lifetime. African American women leaders developed confidence and a sense of self-worth through the Civil Rights Movement and their contributions, which allowed them to continue lifelong development in their personal and professional lives. Early grounding in black culture and recognition of their cultural heritage helped them develop effective coping mechanisms. Their individual growth and dedication to improving the lots of black people were natural consequences of their personal circumstances and philosophy.

The courage these women manifested did not preclude fear. They grappled with known dangers and demonstrated remarkable courage in accepting the uncertain and sometimes dangerous consequences of their leadership. Myrlie Evers's family home was firebombed, and she lived with the threat of bombing and assassination. Diane Nash recounts that several freedom riders gave her sealed envelopes to be mailed in the event of their deaths. Kathleen Cleaver was targeted by the FBI. Judy Richardson and SNCC were constantly under attack and threat of attack. Despite the danger, these women persevered.

African American women's leadership is compassionate and loving. When Mamie Till Bradley, the mother of slain teenager Emmett Till, expressed sympathy and love for the children of those who killed her son, she spoke passionately and eloquently about the values of redemption, forgiveness, and peace. Bradley's choice to display the mutilated body of her son was a bold move of adaptive leadership. Forgiveness, as exemplified by Bradley—as well as by both Martin Luther King and Coretta Scott King—is assertive and powerful. Those extending forgiveness exhibit moral authority and grace.

The Women of *Lighting the Fires of Freedom*

In *The Bone and Sinew of the Race,* Carole Marks (1993) writes of the "heroic sacrifice" of black women household workers (p. 165). Whether sharecroppers like Fannie Lou Hamer or professionals like teacher Jo Ann Robinson, black women have borne burdens, been committed activists, and dreamed worlds where others might have opportunities that they themselves might not enjoy.

My mother was one of these women. An extraordinarily intelligent, talented, and beautiful woman, she spent much of her life—from the 1940s to the 1960s—working as a maid in households or motels. Her migration to Erie, Pennsylvania, in the mid-1940s—where I was born in 1946—had taken a circuitous path from a small town in Arkansas. Her formal education was cut short because the closest high school that blacks could attend was in Little Rock, one hundred miles away. Outside of her work life, my mother—like many other black women of her era—was an elegant, refined person of great vision who was viewed as a leader in the community. She personified a "servant leader." She was active in supporting neighbors in need and in our schools—which our family essentially integrated. As a community leader, my mother created an informal network to assist our neighbors in obtaining food and other basic necessities, purchasing or bartering for food and then giving it to those in greater need than our immediate family. She was not a part of any formal organization. Partly because we were poor, my mother was not invited to be part of women's social clubs. She was not active in church either. My mother deemed church hypocritical and too formal. She also knew that there was something wrong with an institution that elevated men while the women did much of the work. Society was not yet using words such as "patriarchal" or "sexist," but she clearly understood power dynamics between the sexes and did her best to change those dynamics or to work around them when change was not yet possible.

I withdrew from Howard University in my sophomore year and became involved in the Civil Rights Movement in 1966, working primarily in Virginia and Tennessee, with some activities in Mississippi, Georgia, Alabama, and Arkansas. My mother bought me a car to use, stretching far beyond her means to give me a better car than she had ever owned. She had to take on additional work to pay for that extraordinary gift. Although she disagreed with my decision to withdraw from Howard University—a monumental choice, given that I attended on a full academic scholarship and we both believed in the power of education to transform lives—she was still determined to help me, and the Movement, in any way she could. She was committed to change and sacrificed to make it happen. While working in Washington, D.C., I enrolled in Antioch College to complete my undergraduate degree. Earning that degree was the fulfillment of the unspoken sacred oath I made to my mother. This book and my doctoral research grew out of my passion to honor the lives of African American women leaders as I have honored my mother, by presenting their stories of courage and purpose—in their own words. I am extraordinarily pleased that they allowed me to keep their lyricism, cadences, and colloquialisms intact. These are real people, sharing real lives.

Like my mother, the women in *Lighting the Fires* recognized and analyzed the role of race in American society and set out to make a difference; they did not seek fame or fortune; they sought a more just world for themselves and their families.

Leading the Fight for Justice

The nine women in *Lighting the Fires of Freedom*, Leah Chase, June Jackson Christmas, Aileen Hernandez, Diane Nash, Judy Richardson, Kathleen Cleaver, Gay McDougall, Gloria Richardson, and Myrlie Evers, represent many others living lives of meaning and worth, to quote Derrick Bell. They answered the call for freedom, showing courage, commitment, and passion. They were principled and steadfast. They lit the fires and showed the way. All of these women continued to serve after the height of their civil rights involvement—not only the broader black community but the nation as a whole. They were actively involved in social justice movements and activities. They embody the lyrics in Sweet Honey in the Rock's "Ella's Song" by Dr. Bernice Johnson Reagon: "We Who Believe in Freedom Cannot Rest Until It Comes."

The indomitable Elaine R. Jones, a native of Norfolk, Virginia, in 1970 became the first African American woman to graduate from the University of Virginia School of Law and the first woman president and director-counsel of the NAACP Legal Defense and Educational Fund (LDF). She says of black women in the Civil Rights Movement, "The point is that no one did what we do. Black women believe in fundamental fairness. We know the difference between right and wrong; that is a way of finding our way and inspiring others."

Harriet Tubman reportedly said that she could have freed more slaves if only they knew they were slaves. The women leaders of the Civil Rights Movement recognized that their individual successes did not separate them from the shared fate of the black community in general. They knew that no matter how good they were, American society did not view them as equals to whites. They acknowledged the burdens of racism and sexism to rid themselves of mental slavery and to motivate themselves to fight for freedom. Their stories speak to their courage and commitment.

Above: Willie Mae Brooks (Neal), the author's mother, in 1946, the year of the author's birth. Below: Sufronia McKnight, the maternal grandmother of the author. Date unknown. Photos courtesy of the author.

Leah Chase, master chef of New Orleans, Louisiana, in the kitchen of Dooky Chase restaurant in the civil rights era. Undated. (Credit: Leah Chase)

1

LEAH CHASE

Born in 1923, Leah Chase has seen many societal changes in her lifetime and played her part in helping to bring about change simply by doing what she does best: bringing people together over good food and providing an atmosphere of warmth and caring. During the Civil Rights Movement, she hosted Martin Luther King Jr., Thurgood Marshall, members of the Student Nonviolent Coordinating Committee, and many others of all races and backgrounds at her family restaurant Dooky Chase in New Orleans. Her interracial gatherings were by their very nature in defiance of the South's segregation laws. Remarkably, the restaurant was not raided or shut down for her then-illegal activities, perhaps because she and her family were held in such high regard by their community, or perhaps because of New Orleans's independent spirit, exemplified by the Cajun French expression *laissez les bons temps rouler* (let the good times roll). The New Orleans spirit sometimes obscures the racism and inequality that simmers beneath the surface; it is a city of contradictions.

Chase did not start off wanting to be a celebrated chef and community leader. She simply started working in what was then her husband's parents' restaurant. Starting as hostess, then working her way up to chef, Chase is now known as the Queen of Creole Cuisine. She achieved that appellation through hard work and a dedication to providing for black people the same elegance and service given by the finest white-owned, white tablecloth restaurants that rejected black people as customers but eagerly hired them as waiters and for other service positions.

When Hurricane Katrina almost destroyed her business, she made the decision to stay and rebuild in her community. Eighty-two years old in 2005, she lived for a while in a trailer provided by the Federal Emergency Management Agency. When the floods came, her son was able to save the valuable African American art collection that she had amassed. Chase built her art collection not in the spirit of a collector, but as a gift to the community. When the restaurant was restored post-Katrina, Chase's art once again took its place on the walls—where it is today.

My interview with Chase took place in her restaurant, where—at age ninety—she was still cooking in the kitchen. We had an unexpected but memorable additional experience, because she was receiving a special commendation from Pope Benedict XVI for her dedicated service. Her faith fuels her energy, and she always answers to a higher authority. She is the inspiration for the character Princess Tiana in Disney's 2009 film *The Princess and the Frog*. Chase is indefatigable and sat for an extended interview without taking offered breaks.

We Changed the Course of America over a Bowl of Gumbo

I think the Movement influenced everybody. People my age, we were a bit frightened about it. It was so different from what we were trying to do. For instance, we were working with the NAACP, trying to work in the system, abide by the rules. Don't offend this one. Don't offend that one. And get it done. But then here comes the young people in the Movement, and they said, "No. We gonna do this." And we thought, "Oh, God, what are they gonna do? What are they gonna do?" People my age were kinda frightened. We didn't know what was gonna happen.

Sometimes we were not as supportive as what we should've been. For instance, Oretha Castle Haley, there's a street named after her now. She was big in the Civil Rights Movement here. She and her sister and a lotta people were big in the Movement. They would go out and go to jail. And her mother, Virgie, worked here at the restaurant. Her mother worked here as a bartender for some forty-some years. Wonderful woman. You know, she didn't understand the Movement just like I didn't understand, because Virgie was a little younger than I. But her children were there, and her children were goin' to jail. It hurt her badly, but she was very supportive. I always admired her for that. Even though she may have been afraid, she may have been this, that, the other, she was very supportive of those children and what they did. Sometimes we'd say, "Oh, Virgie, they're goin' to jail. What are we goin' to do?" And all this kind of thing. But she was supportive where sometimes we were frightened by it, you know?

I'd listen in on the meetings and what they had to do. I said, "Oh my goodness, they gonna get in trouble." They gonna do this and they gonna do that. But they did it. And it really taught me a lesson: sometimes you have to just bam those down, you know? And just take care of it after that. Now, we worked in the NAACP trying to do this, trying to do that. That movement was just too slow. Now that I look back at it, it would've never gotten done. We would've been here 'til today trying to work within the system. Sometimes to get things done, you have to just bam, do it.

Sometimes we opened doors and we were not ready for what was behind those doors. And that is because we didn't know. All those things, those people, we looked at 'em as, "Oh, they're so radical." But they were true to what they did, and they were sincere about their work, and they worked at it. All those things helped us move to where we are today. If they hadn't done their jobs or what they had to do, we wouldn't be here today.

I don't think people my age were supportive enough of those young people. Now, that's my belief. Because after that movement, we lost a lot of our young people. They were not conforming to society. They were going off, going to jail. They were radical people. I feel if people my age were more supportive and said, "Look, you do this but we gotta come back now. We have to do this and do that," and put 'em on another track, I think it would've been better. That's just my feeling. I think we should've been better, you know, than they takin' all the whippin' and do the things that they did.

But sometimes you make progress by offending some people. You're not gonna please everybody, but you have to move on. Somebody's gonna get hurt maybe, but that's life. And that's somethin' that's gone on for years. You know, way back in the day in the biblical days, they were trying to make changes and do this. You're gonna hurt somebody, but that's progress. You figure, well, I don't know what tomorrow's gonna bring, but I have to do what I have to do today. And tomorrow will take care of tomorrow. So you just go on believin' that and doing that. You disagree with people along the way, but you support 'em. That's all I did.

They would come here, and we would feed them, and they would plan their meetings. We had a room upstairs at that time where they would plan all their meetings. Then they would go out. Some would go through Mississippi and got put in jail, had all kinds of things happen to them. Then they would come back. My job was to feed them all the time and let 'em have this place to meet.

I didn't think I was doing anything brave. I just thought I was doing what I was supposed to do. It was nothing glorious. I just knew I had to feed 'em. When they would come here for meetings, my job was to feed them. It was always gumbo and fried chicken. Always a bowl of gumbo. Over a bowl of gumbo, you can really talk it over and change a whole lot of things.

When I think back, in some ways we changed the course of America over a bowl of gumbo. Because people planned what they were gonna do—they were gonna do this, they were gonna change, and they were gonna do different things. "Are we gonna sit in here," or, "Are we gonna take over this place," and all this kind of thing, whiles they had that bowl of gumbo.

I really think a lot can be done over food today. When you're dealing with other countries, I think if we just sat down and talked about it over some dinner, maybe we could do better things. We did that in the Civil Rights Movement.

The Way We Lived in This City

If you notice, in this city, things went a little smoother than it went, for instance, in Mississippi, you know? We didn't have all the big boycotts that they had. I think it's the way we lived in this city. In this city, blacks didn't live on one side of town and whites on another side like you had in many cities you went to. You would go to a side where it was all black people.

Here in this city, right here in this building here, you had maybe a black person living here, a white person living next door. Now you didn't associate with them. You didn't go out. You were not their friends. You talked to them every day, and that's as far as it went. I think a lot of the hurt and the harshness came because really, we didn't know the whites in other places, they didn't know us. If you know somebody, then you tend to be able to work with them a little better. I think because people knew one another in this city that it worked out good.

We had no black policemen way back in those days. We had only white policemen. My mother-in-law was living then, and she had just a little front shop downstairs. You had policemen. This was their beat. This was the area they worked. So my mother-in-law would say, "Well, when it's our lunchtime, we'll give you a sandwich." It wasn't a bribe with her. Of course you can't do that today. It would be called bribery and all this kind of stupidness. It was just a kind deed. You gonna work to protect my neighborhood, I'm gonna give you a sandwich. And the policemen were white. So when we had people here at the restaurant, they didn't bother us. I think it made it easier.

That just may be my imagination, or maybe the whites handled it differently. You know, people can think one way and work another way. I always think you have to be cautious of that person. I remember Shirley Chisholm came down here when she was running for president. She said to me one day, "You know, Leah, up in New York in the North and the Northeast and all, whites will tell you one thing and pretend that—'I like you, this, that, and the other.' And it is not so." She said, "But what I like about the southern whites, they will tell you point blank, 'I can't vote for you because you're black.'" And she admired that. She said, "Now I can deal with that. You tell me point blank, 'I like your program. I like you. I like what you do. But I'm not gonna vote for you just because you're black.'" She appreciated that honesty, or that brashness, or whatever it was, rather than pretend you're one thing and then do another.

So, maybe we had some pretense here in New Orleans. Maybe they pretended. But we tended to work together. On every corner were Italians. We had Italian groceries on every corner, and they lived over their grocery store. They lived upstairs, and the grocery store was downstairs. So they knew the community, and they worked with the community. We don't have that anymore.

Whites wanted your vote. I think it was politics most of the time. It was the political system. You know, when you were able to vote, they wanted that vote. And they wanted you to vote for them. So they had no other place to meet with you other than some church or here. So they would meet here. You would see the black ministers and all that meet with the people runnin' for mayor, runnin' for whatever they were runnin' for. We had a dining room upstairs, and they would meet up there all the time to get your vote and to see if you could get your people to vote for them. It was a political thing, more or less. The mayor himself—Chep Morrison was the mayor then—would meet here to meet with people and to talk it over with people. How that came about, I may never know.

I'll never forget Jim Dombrowski. Jim Dombrowski was an old man who founded the Highlander Folk School. Rosa Parks came out of Highlander. They trained you in passive resistance, taught you how to do things, change the system easy and all that kind of thing. Jim Dombrowski would come here, and he was working mostly with labor unions, trying to integrate labor unions. So we would have Jim and all the labor people here. And they were just here. Nobody bothered 'em, you know? They would meet here. Nobody ever did 'em anything. It was just done. I've had everybody. Everybody would come here.

My father-in-law was really respected in the community. People loved him. He was a people person. My mother-in-law was the same way. So I guess they knew them, you know? And they just didn't give us any trouble. Only one time we had a bomb. A pipe bomb thrown through the front door. That was by a passing car, don't know what. And you would get ugly letters in the mail, things in the mail that were ugly notes. But that was it. We didn't have any other problems here. Now, why? I'll never, ever know why in New Orleans we just didn't have all of that.

I Wasn't Going in a Sewing Factory

I came up so poor, with nothing. I'm talkin' nothing. We had nothing. My mother would get clothes, people would give her coats, and she would make us rip 'em up and turn them over, and she would make it on the wrong side. So you see, we had a new coat. It was on the wrong side. But we had all of that. We had basic foods to eat. Sometimes it was just grits or just nothin', but you had it. You were never hungry. You had food to eat because you grew it in the country. You had beans without meat. Never had meat. Maybe on Sundays if you could afford it. But that didn't kill you. You had some unity in your family. You had the family there. And you just went on. So I always tell 'em, like Langston Hughes says in "Mother to Son," "Life for me ain't been no crystal stair." But it was really good.

I graduated from high school here in New Orleans, Saint Mary's Academy, when I was sixteen years old. I was only sixteen. I graduated in May, and I had turned sixteen in January. So I was young. I was really too young. In those days you couldn't get anything done until you were eighteen.

So I went back to Madisonville, a little town across the lake where I grew up. And all I had to do was housework. Clean up for people, wash clothes or cook, or do whatever in houses. I just didn't wanna do that all of my life. I didn't have money. I was the top of the line. My mother had fourteen children. She raised eleven of us. I'm the top of the line of all those children. So I had to get out and work so they could get at least high school—you know, at least high school. Now that I go back, from this small town I may have been the first one in my group to get a high school education.

You would get out of school, and if you were a girl, you just hung around and worked in the houses like I did, and then got married. But my mother was from New Orleans, and she believed in education. My father, as country as he was, he agreed with my mother.

He agreed with her that you had to read, you had to study. So when my mother said I was going to high school in New Orleans, that was okay with him.

So I came here to go to high school. Then after high school, there was no work at home, so I had to come here to work. Now that was a whole different ball game because all the so-called *Creoles de couleur*, the Creoles of color, worked in sewing factories. They had any number of sewing factories in New Orleans. They made pants. They made suits. They made shirts. All kind of sewing factories. That's where the women worked. I wish we had that today, but we don't. Because that would give women work.

But when I came, I guess I was militant, because I wasn't going in a sewing factory. I could sew, because we were taught to sew, but I couldn't see myself shootin' out pants pockets all day long, and that's what you did in the sewin' factory. It was what they called "piecework." Either you made the pockets, you set the pockets, or you made the flies on the pants, or you set the flies on the pants. Then at the end, you had a whole pant. But I couldn't do that. So I went to work . . . in the French Quarter. Oh, God. That was a ridiculous thing to do—so they thought. But I liked it. I liked waiting tables, and I liked the people I saw. It was a mixture of people, more white than black.

Whatever it was, I liked it, you know? I went to work for a dollar a day at first, would you believe? But then you made tips. You could go home with about seven, eight dollars a day. Back then, in 1940, that was pretty good. That was pretty good. My mother and my daddy never disagreed with me for doing that. They never did. But my aunts, they all thought that was ridiculous. That I should be, you know, makin' pants or sewin' in a factory. But I learned a lot in the French Quarter. At the restaurant I worked at, I learned what to do, what to buy, and how to do it. I learned to love this business.

Dooky Chase

Now, when I met Dooky he was only eighteen years old. He was a musician. But he had been with a big band since he was in grammar school, would you believe? He had a seventeen-piece band, a big band when he was sixteen years old.

So he was out here in the music world. When I met him, I hated musicians. Thought they were the craziest things I ever saw. I liked people like athletes, like boxers. Boxing was big in those days. Baseball, big in those days. I saw physical and emotional strength. I like people with physical strength. I like people with emotional strength. But musicians didn't ring my bell. I don't know how I came to marry one.

When I married Dooky, his mother and his father had this restaurant. It was just on the corner, just where the bar is now. My mother-in-law, she was unbelievable, the more I think about how she did what she did. She had no knowledge of restaurants as we know them today.

My father-in-law had ulcers and he was sick. He was what we call here in this area a "lottery vendor." What you would call in your area "numbers runner." But we're very sophisticated in the South. We would say, "We're not numbers runners. We are lottery vendors, my dear. It's a business." And that's where he made his money. Selling lottery and doing lottery in those days. So, you had your clients that would play these gigs every day. They would wait for you to come, and you would go to their houses and collect their money every day.

After my father-in-law got so sick and he couldn't go out, he couldn't do that anymore. So my mother-in-law opened up this little shop. It was across the street at that time. She made sandwiches and he could write the lottery inside of the little shop. He wouldn't have to go on the street anymore. So that's how she started in this business. My mother-in-law was a good money manager. I am not.

She knew how to get that bottom line, you know? She knew if she bought this what she should make on that. And she built it. When I came in here in '46, it was just fried food and the bar and all that. But she was makin' money.

Well, in the forties, it was good. You know, Depression was over. People were makin' money. People were workin'. Before that, it was terrible, you know? The Great Crash was what, 1929? I was born in '23, so I was six years old. So that didn't get over 'til what, '40? You had ten years of that poverty. Ten years. So when the war came and people were makin' money, everybody was really happy, and she could really do things.

Let Me Just Serve It Nice

I always wanted in the black community what I saw whites had. A good restaurant, a fine restaurant with tablecloths and napkins and nice glasses. I thought our people deserved that. We had nothin' for so long. So when we come out, we deserve just what you have. I oughta be able to give you just what Commander's Palace in the Garden District gives you. I oughta do that. I can serve my greens and my pork chops or whatever, and my chicken. But let me serve it up on a pretty plate. Let me serve it with a napkin. Let me just serve it nice.

When I came here in '46, I was workin' in the French Quarter. So I said, "Oh no. We gonna do just like they did. We gonna set these tables up." And they'd say, "Oh no. We can't set these tables 'cause who's gonna eat with these forks that been sittin' on the table?" I said, "Well, they do it over there. They sit those forks on that table."

Because during the segregation, in this city and in this area, parents didn't tell you why you couldn't sit. I think in Mississippi, they told their children, "You can't eat there because you're black." You know what they would tell us? "Oh no, you don't wanna eat there. No, all those people were drinking out the same glass. You do not wanna do that. You don't wanna eat there. It's not clean." And it was clean. But that was their way of protecting you here.

So we knew we couldn't eat there because we were black, but they never told us that. They didn't tell us that. They covered it up. Or, "You can't sit in this fine seat in the theater. It's not good anyway. Because look how much better you can see if you're sitting up high." And I'll never forget: "I wanna sit down there. I wanna sit down there. It looks good down there." "No, you can see better up here." Those are the kind of things they did to shelter you in those days around this area. So you see, we just felt sheltered.

You would go out. You were not allowed to drink. They would tell you, "Wait 'til you get home." You didn't drink in the street. You didn't eat in the street. Wait until you get home. So that was the thing I liked about Mardi Gras. When Mardi Gras came, it was all right to eat and drink in the street. I thought that was the biggest fun going, to be able to have a Coke or somethin' while you were walkin' in the street, you know? Because we were not allowed to do that. They sheltered us more in this area, I think. It was strange. I can't figure it out.

You see, then, blacks were eating in their homes. Because I told you, they would never eat out because they thought it wasn't clean and this, that, and the other. And they had no nice places. They would come here on the weekend, particularly, because they knew my mother-in-law and they knew my father-in-law, and they would come and sit down and have some drinks. To accompany those drinks, they would have food. So they would have chicken or they would have fried oysters, what they didn't have at home. But most of the time they cooked everything at home. So when I came in here, I said, "Oh no. We gonna change this." And this was so stupid and naïve.

I came out of the Quarters, and here we were serving fried oysters and fried things. "Oh," I said. "No, we have to do things differently." I said, "The only difference in people is the color of their skin. I'm gonna start doing with the cream sauces what I saw them do in the Quarters in the white restaurants." Because they ate more French cooking, like they would do Newburg sauces and all kinda cream sauces and those kinda things. So I'm gonna put that on. I'm gonna put lobster thermidor. Oh, God. The black people said, "Oh, she is goin' crazy." They told my mother-in-law, "She's gonna ruin your business. All the things that you worked for, she's gonna ruin them, you know? By her changes. What she's gonna do?" Then you learn.

We have different cultures, which is good. If you're German, you want good German food. If you're Italian, you want that. If you're black, you want what you want, and you want your food that you're accustomed to eating. You see, here I am. I'm just twenty-two, twenty-three years old. So I'm learning. Hey, wait a minute. You're stupid. Different cultures. People like what they like. So I had to back up, I had to start makin' things that I knew they liked. Chicken breasts stuffed with oyster dressin', veal panéed, what they had all the time. Shrimp Creole. The things that people were accustomed to. Now I find, hey, the whites come here. They know what I serve. They come here for what I serve.

I can do the cream sauces. I can do anything you want me to do. But I look at my customer and what he wants. That's what they come here for, for what I serve here. And they will bring their guests. They will say, "Well, we goin' here tonight." Then blacks will tell you, and I like to hear them say that, "Now I'm gonna take you to 'our' restaurant." And it's here. They never referred to this as Dooky Chase's. They would always just say, "We goin' to The Restaurant." That's it. So when you said in the black community, "We're goin' to The Restaurant," you knew where you were comin'. You were comin' here. I had a hard time changin' and gettin' people to understand this is what you do. I love service. I think people deserve good service. No matter what you serve them, I like it done well.

Now, after integration—and I don't know what you think about integration, but for me, it was the best thing in the world—you taught people. People learned a lot. You know, you had all these people, blacks here, whites here, never minglin'. So you never knew what went on in the white restaurants. You didn't know how to eat all this crème brûlée and these cream sauces. Here comes integration. Then you get to learn about that. Now I can serve you anything. Look how terrible that was to keep all these people from learning. And that kept them from growing. See, when you learn things, you can grow.

That, to me, is the best thing about integration, is you learn different things. You learn things that you were not accustomed to because you were never allowed to do that. You were never allowed to go places where you saw these things. We were not allowed in the museum. So look what you missed. Look what all these people missed, and all the community missed. Look what a powerhouse of people you would've had, had you done like John McDonogh.* Maybe say, "I'm gonna educate these people. I'm gonna train them. I'm gonna teach 'em things." But you didn't do that. So they didn't have that knowledge of arts and things to make their life prettier and to make their lives better. That was the saddest thing about segregation, not necessarily who you sit next to. Wasn't important who you sat next to—"Oh, if you could sit here!"—as you were missing out on learning everything.

Putting It Up on the Wall

I had a friend, and I'll never forget her. She's dead now. Celestine Cook. She was the first African American to sit on the board of the New Orleans Museum of Art. The black community didn't grasp on that, what she was all about. They thought, you know how we

---

*McDonogh, a real estate speculator and slaveholder, left his fortune to fund public schools in New Orleans and Baltimore. More than thirty schools in the New Orleans public school system at one time bore the McDonogh name.

are: "Oh, you just wanna be Miss Society," or, "You just wanna be uppity," that kind of stupidness. But she was really trying to teach other people. So when she came to me, I am runnin' this, workin' my kitchen, doin' that. And she said, "It's my turn to rotate." After three years, you rotate off the board. She said, "And I'm gonna put your name up."

I said, "Oh, is she gonna put my name up? They're not gonna take me on there. I don't know anything." I have no college education. I'm just a high school graduate, and I don't have this and I don't have that. I said, "Don't do that. Because I don't know one thing about art, Celestine. I don't know anything about it. I have never set foot in the inside of a museum in my life. So I don't know that." Okay, so she said, "But you don't know what it's gonna do for your business," that's what she told me. "It's gonna do wonders for your business." So I said, "Okay." That's what I'm all about, trying to make this restaurant grow, trying to make it a name place to go.

That was 1977. When she put my name up, my name came up tied with a very prominent Jewish man. I don't know if you know the works of Ida Kohlmeyer, very famous Jewish woman who was an artist in this area. She's now dead. But her work is still all over the place around here. It was her brother-in-law. I came up tied with Mr. Kohlmeyer. Now, to break the tie, that means the chairman of the board has to vote. He was a prominent Jewish lawyer in this city. And Mr. Steeg voted for me. I always thanked this man 'til the day he died. I always admired him for that, because that took vision. That took guts to vote for me in those times in the seventies. I had nothing and you're turnin' down a man with money, a man with knowledge of the arts, a man with everything, and you gonna vote for me as a black woman? That was vision. He knew that somewhere along the way, you had to lift these people up. You had to make a difference. You had to do that. I never forgot him for that.

I sat on that board and I learned. Celestine was so gung-ho. She was the one who got the first African American to show in that museum, to have an exhibition. It was Jacob Lawrence. So she said, "Leah, now come on. You come see this exhibit." I said, "Celestine, I am not gonna know a bloomin' thing about this. I don't know anything about art." I'd dress up to go to the museum. I put on my best dress and a nice little fur cape I had, nice. That's how stupid I am. I think you gotta dress up to go to the museum. I think you got to be elegant to go to the museum. So I went and I sat there. I sat in that audience, and I said I'm not gonna know one thing this man is talking about. I'm just gonna sit here like a dummy and listen. But when Jacob Lawrence began to talk about his work, I realized I could relate to him. I could relate to what he was talkin' about because we came up the same way, poor, strugglin' to do what we had to do.

I'll never forget Jake, and we became good friends after that. I learned a lot. So then I started collecting work by African Americans. Because in those days, African Americans had no way to show their work. They had no place. The galleries were not showing African American art. Now, it's crazy. They are buying up everything. So I started putting it up on the wall. That was controversial in my community. "You're not a museum," and "Nobody's gonna like this stuff." I said, "But I like it, and I'm just gonna put it up there. I like it."

Even my husband, he pitched a fit when we did this big thing you see there by Bruce Brice, that big collage over there? With all the Indians? Because black people in this area were clannish. You know, they didn't wanna be a part of what wasn't really their way of living. That was them. You are what you are. But they didn't wanna be a part of the Mardi Gras Indians, the dances on the street and all that. So I had a big fuss about puttin' that work up there. So when I put it up there, and we opened this place, oh God, all the whites who knew about art, they flocked over there to see this. They thought it was just marvelous.

I'm proud to say and to know that since I've put all this art out, black people now don't go to the stores and buy art that matches the sofa. It doesn't have to match the sofa, it just has to talk to you. You could put it anywhere. I learned to put it everywhere. I was tryin' to put all my big boys together, like the Jake Lawrence, John Biggers, and the Elizabeth Catletts—the big guys, I put them together. I got this gold room. You have some John Biggers. You have some of my granddaughter's work. You have some of this. You have the folk art and all that kind of thing. One lady came in here, and I said, "But look at that room. It is crazy the way the art is hung." I said, "It's just a mess." She said, "No, Leah. That's what you call 'salon hanging.'" I said, "Well, very good. I got a salon in there." So you learn. You learn.

I'm so proud that other people learn. It's all about learning. It's all about teaching people. What little you know, pass it on. You have to pass it on. And they'll take it and somebody else'll make it grow. That's what I do in the arts, and I like it. I served my time on the board. Now I am an honorary life member on the board. I do a lot of fundraising. Last year, my birthday party was a big fundraiser at the museum, and I raised $100,000. They had an exhibition that a young artist did of me in my kitchen. So, people learn to see you as you are. You are just what you are. And you can make a difference by just being who you are.

Your Work on Earth Is What You Do for Other People

You can work in the total community, and I worked the total community. I will give to this white organization. I will give to this Jewish organization. I go for the total community. I feel good about that because then people come together and they learn to help you. They have helped me get this whole restaurant back up after the storm. I lost everything but the art on the wall, and that was moved off by some firemen who helped my grandchildren take it off the wall. The water was two feet up to that chair rail.

After Katrina, 80 percent of this city was underwater. It was terrible. But the thing that hit me the hardest was when I went out to City Park and I saw those great oaks that were two hundred years old down. How do you put a tree up again? You can build a house. You sure can't build a tree overnight. The loss of those mighty oaks just floored me. We saved some, but some are just gone. That showed me the power of that mighty being. What is this power so great that it would take this oak, this two-hundred-year tree, up? We have to believe there's a bigger power than us, and we cannot control that big power. We just have to learn to do what we have to do and live. Because you just have no control over that. Those are the things that just keep you goin'. You just pray and keep goin'. I didn't consider myself very brave. I just lived. You know, you just go from day to day. I do things that same way now. I pray a lot. And you know, we as black people do pray a lot.

I woulda lost everything. I usually do fundraising. I would go all around Fort Wayne, Indiana. I would go help them fundraise and start their food bank. You meet people. That's what I tell people, you know? Give a little. Do a little charity work. Work with other people. It's not about you. It's not all about earnin'. My mother always taught us that your job on earth is what you do to feed your face, what you do to get paid to take care of you. But your work on earth is what you do for other people. I never forgot that. So I always try to do whatever I can do to help other people. After the storm, Fort Wayne sent me a check for $30,000 to buy all those chairs. People came from all over. Starbucks came to the tune of $149,000 to help me get up.

You know, I never paid attention to money that much. Maybe I should have, saving it or putting it on the sides for what they call a rainy day. I was not good at that. I would tend to maybe spend more money on things that I think are important. I would give to people my last dollar. My husband always said that. I said, "Oh, I wish I would win the lottery." He said, "What would you do with it? It wouldn't do you any good. You'd give it away." I'd say, "Well, I would be happy to give it away. I'd have it to give away."

Money never fazed me. I don't like to look at money, for instance. I like what money can buy, and what money can get for you. But to look at a stack of money? My mother-in-law used to like to look at a stack of money. She carried a roll in her bosom every day she set out. She would roll those out and she might be walkin' around with $500 in her bosom every day. Now that? Nuh-uh. No, I couldn't do that. I'm not that interested in the sight of money. I want what money will buy. I want what money will do for you, will get you somethin' else or will get somebody else somethin' else. That's how I feel about money. It's like the man says in *Hello, Dolly*, "Money is like manure. It's not worth a thing unless it's spread around, encouraging young things to grow." That's the way I feel. Money is made to spread around.

I joke all the time, I said, "If they wanted you to hold on to money, they wouldn't have all those ugly men on it anyway." Nothin' pretty about George Washington. Nothin' pretty about Abraham Lincoln, Ben Franklin. None of them good-looking men. You know, if they put Bill Clinton on there, Obama on there, maybe I'll save a few. Who wants a bunch of old men hangin' around? Money is made to make things grow, make the community grow. You spread it around, and that's how it is.

I didn't spread it around as much as I could have if I had more access to it. People doubt that. They don't understand. This business, I worked to make it what it is today. But either it was my mother-in-law who controlled the money, or my husband who controlled the money. Sometimes I look at it and I say maybe I should've done different. You know, now that I'm older, maybe I should've gotten more for myself. That was never on my mind. Til today, it's what I can do to better this business.

I tell that to young people. If you gonna go to work, never mind what your pay is. Do your job. The money will be there. If you gonna

wait on these tables, don't think about that tip, think about that
service. The tip will be there. See, you put first things first, put
the work first, and then don't worry about the money. It's gonna be
there. It's gonna come. Daddy used to say, "Don't worry about anything, because worry don't help you at all." Just go from day to day
doing the best you can do, and do what you can do, and always help
others. It's gonna work out for you. It worked out for me.

I'm grateful for what you're doing. Because young people have to
read these things. I tell them all the time. Oh, they gonna march on
Martin Luther King's birthday, they gonna celebrate, and they gonna dance. I said, "But you forgot one thing, Martin Luther King died
for you to work." He died for you to get good pay for your work. Now
you're getting good pay for your work. We're paying the dishwasher
$10.00, $10.50 an hour. So you gettin' fair pay for your work. So
please work. That, to me, is how I do in honor of King, in honor of
Malcolm X, in honor of Medgar Evers. Work. Do for others. That's
what those people died for.

The three women I really most admired in my life were Coretta
King, Myrlie Evers, and Betty Shabazz. First, you know, I met
Coretta King. Of course, Coretta had an education. When Martin
was out here, she was already educated. Myrlie Evers wasn't. Betty
Shabazz wasn't. They had to get themselves educated and take care
of their children. Those three women, I don't know how in the
world they did what they did. You're gonna kill my husband. Or
my husband's gonna die for you and leave me with these children,
and you're not doin' better? I would be mean and ugly. They were
not. They were not bitter. They had no hate in their souls for anybody, even for their own people. I would be mad at my own people.
Look! My husband died, left me with the children. And what are
you doing? You're not doing what you're supposed to do. I would get
furious. I would be angry and I would be bitter. No, they were not.

I know I couldn't do what those three women did. They just carried on their lives and raised their children. To me that was remark-

able. When I saw this funeral they gave Coretta, I thought, "So deserved." Because this woman had to support these men. They got women who did things, Dorothy Height and all these women, but these three women just did what they had to do. They were amazing. I don't know how you get that much courage. I saw Myrlie at the president's second inauguration. Oh, I was so proud. She looked so beautiful.

When you write these stories, young people should let that soak in and say, you are what you are today because somebody else laid the groundwork for you. Somebody died for you to get this far. So you may not have to die for it, but please do something to uplift somebody else. I tell 'em, "Pick up your pants and go to work." These people will not have died in vain if you just do what you have to do. And that's all you have to do. But you got to remember those things, and you don't harp on 'em, you don't stay there in that spot and mourn over it and groan over it. You do like those three women I'm talkin' about did. You just move on. You'll be taken care of. Don't worry about it. Don't worry about what your next dress is. Nobody cares anyway. Nobody cares what kinda shoes you have on. Nobody cares anything, but if you do what you have to do, they care about you. That's the most important thing.

We have a good city with good people in this city. We gonna have some that's gonna do wrong, but then when you think about it, we allow them to do wrong. We put politicians in office and leave 'em stayed too long. They get complacent. We don't pay attention to what they doin' and they go off doin' the wrong things. So we have to do better than that. Think about what the country would be if every man would do just a little bit. So now blacks have the opportunity, take every opportunity there is and help move yourself up. Then you have the power.

We have a community here called the "Lower Nine." They have loads of people there. I tell people who work with these people—their district council people, their congressmen: with people you have power. But you have to help empower them and show them how we gonna make this work. Then you will be a community to reckon with. People will come to you if you doin' what you have to do. That's what your leaders have to do. You put leaders and you expect them to lead you. I tell 'em all the time, "Just tell me what I have to do and I'm gonna do it. Tell me what it takes." You got to go back and you got to say, "I'm gonna help you wherever I can help you." If it's to clean up my streets, if it's to uplift my neighborhood one block at a time.

It's good that people like you write about these things. And you say, "Oh, Lord. Listening to the same thing over and over." But sometimes you listen and then you look at the thing differently. It's just like lookin' at art. I said, "Look, if you don't like what you see the first time, look again." Look again. A little bit differently. It's the same way you look at life. It may look bad one day. It may look terrible. Take another look. Then you gonna see somethin' good. You gonna see something that makes you work.

The same way you look at art, the same way you look at this, that, and the other. You listen to rap music. "I don't like what I hear." Listen again, then you hear the fine meat. You hear the talent it took for them to get this beat just right. Forget the words. Listen to the meat. Look at the good side of it. I think we'll make it. But you just gotta work at it. Don't give up on life. You just keep going. It takes some prayer, and it takes some praise, and it takes some doing.

As my grandson says, and I can punch him every time he says that, "Oh, but Grandmother, it's all good." I said, "No, it's not all good." But it is all good. Just look for the goodness in it. My pastor and bishop came to bring me greetings from the pope. Now I had greetings from the president, from George W. Bush, from Obama, from this one, from that one, but the pope, my goodness. What did I do? Nothing. Who am I? Nobody. So it's been a good life for me. It really worked out for me. And I'm still workin' at it. I'm still trying to make it what I want.

Leah Chase, Louisiana, in the kitchen of Dooky Chase restaurant, April 15, 1986. (Credit: AP Photos)

Dr. June Jackson Christmas speaking at an American Psychiatric Association event the day after students were killed at Jackson State College in 1970. (Credit: Novartis)

2

DR. JUNE JACKSON CHRISTMAS

Born in 1924, June Jackson Christmas grew up in Cambridge, Massachusetts, in the late 1920s and early 1930s. Christmas has faced racism and sexism all her life and in almost every organization with which she has been involved, whether the quintessentially American institutions such as the Girl Scouts and the YWCA or institutions of higher education. She was one of the first African Americans to attend Vassar College; she graduated in December 1944. As a student she championed the cause of Japanese Americans who had been relocated during World War II. Christmas was also a pioneer and leader in the field of psychiatry. She specialized in community mental health care, especially for low-income African Americans, and served as mental health commissioner under three New York City mayors. With her husband, Christmas waged a personal fight against housing discrimination that changed New York City law. I interviewed Christmas in 2011 at her home. The wide-ranging conversation of her activism throughout her life reflects the struggles, triumphs, and indomitability of black America.

The Civil Rights Movement Starts in the Mind

Before the Civil Rights Movement, we were struggling against barriers and doing what black people said: being twice as good as white folks, having high expectations, and trying to live up to them. I've been involved in issues of the struggle to obtain rights, particularly for African Americans, from a young age. I learned from all of this that the Civil Rights Movement starts early and it starts in the mind. It starts in the home, and people have different ways of being part of it.

My parents were both lower-middle-class African Americans who instilled in my younger sister and me a sense of pride and identification with people who had broken barriers. We knew it wasn't easy. When I speak to my grandson, who goes to the Harlem School of the Arts, I say to him, "Dorothy Maynor was a singer back in the late thirties, early forties who later started this school" and say that she was a pioneer as a singer and an operatic soprano. When he wonders why that is so important, I give him a little bit of the history of remembering hearing her sing at Jordan Hall in Boston when I was maybe ten years old.

Though my parents had both only gone to high school, my mother had gone to a high school for practical arts; she became a milliner and a seamstress. At the school, mathematics was a foundation of millinery training. Style and design were incorporated in the program, and arts and history and music were strong foundations. So, as I grew up, she was very much interested in making sure that I had a background in music. I wasn't a very good piano player, so the teacher said, "Maybe June should study elocution." So I did. And as my husband used to say, I haven't stopped talking yet.

My Father

My father came from a family that had been in New England for several generations. His mother, from Maine, she was African

American and Mi'kmaq Indian, and his father's family was from Virginia and Danbury, Connecticut, where one of them was a free man of color in the mid-1800s. They had been in New England for a while but had some connections to the South as well. He too grew up in a family where they valued education, and he graduated from Boys High. His father did not want his four daughters to work in anyone's kitchen, so one went to normal school to become a teacher and married along the way. Another went to clerical school to become a secretary, another did not go on to college as they hoped she would, and another was one of the early black graduates of Radcliffe College, graduating cum laude in 1919.

My father had wanted to become an accountant, a CPA, but his father could not help him financially. My father was always disappointed that he didn't go on to Bentley College of Accounting, but he kept his interest in math. All during the time I was growing up, he had math problems for me. I'd be drying the dishes and he'd be giving me all kinds of problems, even though I wasn't that interested in math.

He had an interest in the arts as well. We went to concerts together. We knew who was breaking down the barriers, particularly in the arts. Roland Hayes, Marian Anderson, Aubrey Pankey, Allan Rohan Crite. Even though we acted as though we had always been in the North, and though the North had never had slavery, we still knew there were barriers. I remember a couple of early incidents that really set me in a fighting mood.

We went to a church in Boston, St. Augustine and St. Martin's Episcopal Church, which had been formed back in the 1880s in the West End, a section of Boston where immigrants from Russia moved later. My paternal grandmother and other black people lived in this part of Boston in the late nineteenth century. When the Russians and other Jewish immigrants moved to this particular area of Boston, black people moved to the South End. That's where my family moved, and the church was broken up because there was no physical presence for it. My great-grandmother Sarah Jackson had the church meet in her living room for a couple of years before they got a little building in the South End. This church was a high church, an Anglican church, that had white priests. All of my father's sisters went there and he was active there as an acolyte.

I remember looking out of the bus on the way to church camp and wondering why the priest was white and all the children were black. Questions occurred to me. Didn't they have black priests in the Episcopalian Church? I knew my grandmother was devoted to this church and I'd heard the story of how it was started in her living room and then they built this building. My family moved from Boston to Cambridge, and when I was about eight years old they started going to another Episcopalian church. I was christened as an Episcopalian, but I later went to this new church in Cambridge. It was a very old, low Episcopalian church, none of this chanting or incense that we had at St. Augustine. I loved this church because it was the church I started going to when I was very young.

Girl Scouts

I became involved with the Girl Scouts through the church. Our troop was predominately white because the church was. Now, even then I was this big do-gooder. I was a Miss Do-It-Right-and-Get-Praise, or as my poor little sister who always got in trouble when I was home would say, I was Miss Goody Two-shoes. So when we had the contest to sell the most cookies for the Girl Scouts, I just knew I was going to win. The prize was going to be a week at the Girl Scout camp where we had all gone on day trips but never for any length of time. I did my best to win, but I didn't win. My friend, who was also black, Clarice Roberts, won. When Clarice won, I went with her to the den mother, Mrs. Glenn, who was the wife of the rector. She said, "Yes, Clarice, you sold more cookies than anyone else. But, I'm sorry, you are not going to get the week at camp." We were surprised. She said, "I'm terribly sorry, you know, we have never had a Negro stay at camp overnight." And we were shocked. I remember hearing for the first time an expression that puzzled me. She said, "That's the lay of the land." When I heard that, I realized that she meant that's how it was. Negro girls couldn't stay at this camp even though one of them had been the best in the contest.

I was angry, upset, and puzzled. I went home to talk to my parents, to ask, "What can I do? How can we fight this?" My father's mother said, "You'll have to figure out if this is one you fight or don't fight." So I began to think, there are some battles you wage and other battles you don't wage. Both my mother and Clarice's mother—my mother went to support Clarice's mother—went to talk to Mrs. Glenn about it, and she reiterated that there was nothing they could do. Since I was in second place, the prize normally would have gone to the second person, but it didn't go to me either. So I guess some white child went for the week. That made an impression. Somehow or other things are not fair. But you don't give up.

YWCA

The other thing that led me to action in Cambridge was that we're talking about the thirties and the YWCA nationally was divided. There were white Ys and black Ys, Negro Ys. When I was in the seventh or eighth grade, a group of us belonged to the YWCA, the Negro Y, that met downtown in Cambridge. The head of the Y at that point was a woman who later went on to become the head of National Y, the internationally known Odile Sweeney. She was head of our little group at the Y. I don't know what we called the club, but it was a club only for Negroes.

When I was eleven or twelve, my friends and I decided we were going to go roller skating. We had heard that the skating rink didn't admit Negroes. We said, "Well, we'll go find out, and we'll see if we can make them admit us." The roller-skating rink was right there on

Massachusetts Avenue in downtown Cambridge, a working-class, business part of Cambridge across the street from the Y. So seven or eight of us went to buy tickets, one after the other, and they said, "No." So we sat down in the area right where the box office was and we said we were going to sit there and we weren't going to leave until they sold us tickets. But, of course, we were very obedient kids. It was Saturday afternoon, and we had to be home by dark. So as time went on, we sat and sat and tried to figure out what to do. We finally said, well, we can't be out if it's really late, so we finally got up, made some kind of stand, and said, "You should be selling tickets to everybody. You shouldn't be selling them to anybody if you're not selling to everybody."

When I got home, my daddy said, "Is that something to be making a fuss about—going roller skating at the rink?" I was a little disturbed because I assumed that he would stand up for it. But he was making the point there are some things you should stand up for and others you don't.

My Father's Struggles in the Post Office

I was in high school when I learned that my father, who had gone to the post office as a laborer and quickly became a clerk, then a supervising clerk, was moving up, but he had only moved up a couple of ranks by the time I was in high school. He was less militant than my mother. My mother belonged at this point, in 1939, to a community relations committee. They both belonged to a community center, which was in the poor black neighborhood, and they were considered middle-class people doing good for other people. They had their own club meetings at this community center that they believed to be beneficial, but they also identified with people who were struggling more.

My father had been taking an exam for promotion each year or two. At the post office back then in the forties, late thirties, the person who got the promotion could come from the top three. Well, Daddy was always in the top three, and he was generally number one, but he never got chosen, always white people. Daddy wasn't going to fight unless he had to. Finally, he determined that he had to fight against discrimination. There weren't that many black people as clerks. There were some black people as laborers. There weren't many black carriers. They were mainly mail sorters. He did protest and, through fighting the system, did eventually get a promotion that he deserved. He went on to become supervisor and then superintendent. When he retired from the post office, he had been superintendent of several post offices.

I've adopted a number of roles from my father and mother. I did get more and more discouraged, then I became encouraged by the Civil Rights Movement. I'm going to fight the system.

My Early Education at School and in Color Consciousness

In high school, I went to Cambridge High and Latin School, a public school. I was on the college track, and I assumed that I was going to be a writer. Those were integrated schools. There were few black kids in the classroom, and I was a very good student; some kids really didn't like me because of that. I was growing up in the age of color discrimination, and I was a dark brown girl among my friends—I was about the brownest among my friends.

My mother was light tan; my sister, caramel color; my father was dark brown like me. I unfortunately took up the idea that if you are going to be brown, or dark brown, you had to be very smart. It was as though being dark brown was a disadvantage and being smart is an advantage. Then I was confused because I found out that being smart could be a disadvantage too. Some people would think, "Oh, she's so smart, she knows all this," then respond with envy and criticism. I kept trying to understand what makes people discriminate against other people within their group because of color. What makes people discriminate against black people as a whole? I decided that one way to figure this out is to become a psychiatrist to help people understand how to get along better.

Friendship in Black and White

At church and at high school, one of my closest friends was white and the other was black. The white girl, Peggy Miller, and I began to do interviews with theater people. In those days, we would often go for the thirty-five-cent ticket to a Saturday matinee and stay around and interview these celebrities for our high school magazine. We started first with autograph collecting. My mother used to talk about going to the theater when she was young and going to see Walter Hampden and Walter Huston and other Shakespearean actors. She spoke about them almost as though she knew them. Peggy and I did this all during high school, and it cemented our relationship and friendship. I knew when I wrote these essays and Peggy and I interviewed people that this was preparing me to be a journalist or psychiatrist.

Theater and Race

Jackie Cooper was one of the early movie people coming out on the stage. I had my autograph book, but I realized maybe we can get an interview with him for the magazine. I was doing fiction for this high school magazine. This would have been in '38 or '39. I'd done a couple of stories in my short story column, won short story contests, and Peggy was a business manager of the magazine. I think some of the people we interviewed, including Orson Welles, were impressed that Peggy and I were young, and we were white and black. We interviewed Oscar Levant, Paul Robeson, Jackie Cooper,

Eddie Bracken, Diosa Costello, Francis Lederer, Don Budge, and Burgess Meredith.

I remember thinking there were no black people working back-stage. It would be just as few as there were at Vassar on campus. There were efforts at fair employment practices back in the late thirties, and there were efforts once the war started to not just inte-grate the armed forces a little bit later but to bring justice at home and civil rights. I would raise those issues when we would be inter-viewing people, if it was appropriate. I remember going out to the Longwood Cricket Club in Boston, in Brookline, and there were no black ball boys. There were no ball girls either. I saw Don Budge maybe three times and interviewed him twice: wasn't it time for Negroes to be in the Tennis Association? His response was some-thing equivalent to well, he didn't get into social issues. Every once in a while, there would be a black artist, like Roland Hayes or Paul Robeson. They would raise issues. "Things have got to improve for Negroes in this country."

Peggy came from an upper-middle-class family, Yankee, and went to the same church as I did. Our parents became friendly, not close. By the time I finished high school, Peggy and my family knew that I was going on to college. Peggy's family knew that a girl from the upper middle class didn't have to go to college—she could get married. My family was a little surprised at this because there were differences of values. Peggy's mother had gone to Wellesley, but she was a widow and couldn't afford to send her daughter off to college. Peggy and I talked about this, and Peggy said she wished she could but she was going to go to secretarial school.

I thought, "What a difference." Here comes someone from an old Yankee family, her mother had gone to college, her late father had gone to college. But the idea was for a white upper-middle-class girl, she's going to get a husband. I assumed I might not even get mar-ried. I'll get a profession.

An Enduring Friendship Across Racial Lines

Peggy and I stayed good friends. I was maid of honor at her wedding; she was matron of honor at mine. She married Sidney Wingate, who was from the South, an army veteran and very lovely person, an engineer she met at MIT. Sadly, she died of cancer twenty-five years ago.

Just recently, I came upon some of the articles she and I wrote for our high school magazine. We were going to write a book after she finished secretarial school and she was working at MIT. She was helpful to me in my getting a job after college in the MIT Radiation Lab. I finished in December because I accelerated—I went three and a half years instead of four. The war began as soon as I started college.

Peggy met her husband at the lab. We also met a writer, Benjamin Miller, a white doctor at Mass General. He was impressed with the fact that we'd remained close friends from the age of Girl Scouts and Brownies and had been in each other's wedding. He said, "Why don't you two write about this?" So Peggy and I decided to write, and all along, in the back of my mind, I was still thinking, "I'm going to be a journalist and a doctor." We started writing chapters of our lives. I would do one chapter, she would do the other. I don't know how many we did, but I found some among the material that I had donated to the Schomburg Center. We didn't finish the book, but we stayed good friends. I was going on to medical school, so I slowed down on the writing, and she was having a family. It would have been an interesting story. Our interracial relationship back then was one that was not common.

Although Peggy never really got involved in protests, she did the right thing. She and her mother were always supportive. Peggy's mother, like mine, was a community relations–type person. "Let us get people to talk together and do things." Peggy wasn't an activist. I became more of an activist as I went off to college. I can't say I didn't see color in our friendship. We knew she was white and I was black. But somehow she was one of those white people who saw beyond race. Whereas, for me, as long as there is racial discrimination, I still see race.

My Path to College

My family assumed that I would apply to Radcliffe. My aunt Geneva graduated there cum laude in 1919. I was second in my class in high school. Yet I didn't know if I could compete at her level, but I still applied to Radcliffe. Then I heard from another girl in Christ Church who was white that her sister, who was at Vassar, had advised her that Vassar had decided to open its doors to Negroes.

I came home and told my mother's mother, Nana, who was dear to my heart and she said, "Oh June, not Vassar. You remember what happened to Anita Hemmings?" I said, "Who's Anita Hemmings?" Well, she said, "She was a girl who went to Vassar and when she got ready to graduate, they wondered if she was a Negro. When they found out she *was*, they didn't let her graduate. She was going to be the valedictorian." I said I had never heard that, and she said, "Yes, that's what happened," and my aunt said the same thing. My mother added, "Do you really want to be away from home?" I said, "Yes. Vassar is changing their policies."

My father at that point was making twenty-one hundred dollars a year in the post office. This was 1941. My mother was not working outside the home then. The war had just started in Europe. At Vassar, tuition and board was twelve hundred dollars for one year. I received a scholarship of six hundred dollars. So my mother and father had to raise the other six hundred dollars. I chose Vassar.

Seeking a Roommate

Before I got to Vassar, I had to fill out a form that said, "Do you want a roommate or not?" Of course, I checked "yes." I assumed that there might not be that many black girls, but I assumed that there might be somebody that I can get along with, black or white. The head of the Vassar Club of Boston wrote me a handwritten note, "Dear June, we noted on the application that you would like to have a roommate, but I think it might be best for you if you don't have a roommate." I knew what that was about, so I said obviously they're writing officially—don't choose a roommate. So I withdrew my request.

I therefore started Vassar assuming that it wasn't going to be all roses, peaches, and cream, if right away they were saying, "Write that you don't want a roommate." I did choose to live in a co-op and discovered, when I got to Vassar, they had had one Negro girl the year before and one other in my year.

Vassar Co-Ops

Being in a co-op at Vassar in 1941, before the war, meant that for one hundred dollars off your board and room, you had to serve as a waiter in the dining room. You made up your beds instead of having the maids make them up. In my second year, I lived in a real co-op, where you got maybe three or four hundred dollars off the board and room. There, you cleaned your own room, made your own beds, cooked your own meals, and did your own dishes. You wiped and put away, and then did a couple of other chores. But you really ran that co-op and took several hundred dollars off your tuition. It was very elite—there were only twenty places, and they were divided among different classes. Because we were a small group, that's where I developed my closest friendships.

The first co-op that I lived in was where Betty McCleary lived, who had entered the year before me as the first openly acknowledged Negro student in Vassar's history. She was interested in medicine, and by now I knew I was interested in medicine too. I used to look upon her as a big sister. But she also wanted to make sure that

I interacted with other people. In addition, Betty looked as though she was Indian and white and a little bit Negro. Only a black person would know she was Negro. She and I did spend a lot of time being asked things together in which we had to explain to white people why black people do this and how black people are not all the same. She was a good big sister.

Years later, I wrote the official history of Negroes at Vassar, "The Black Presence at Vassar College," and it was published in the *Vassar Quarterly*. Somebody wrote me and said, "Dear Dr. Christmas, I think you are mistaken. There was a Negro girl in my class maybe a year or so before Betty McCleary had come, but she stayed only one year."

I got in touch with her, and she said, "Yes, I did go to Vassar maybe a year before Betty McCleary. It was just too oppressive for me. I'm from Ohio, and I couldn't see my parents that often, so I stayed only a year. I want you to know that I thought about you over the years because as you became active in the American Psychiatric Association, my husband, who is a psychiatrist, often wanted to speak to you—he's African American—and to tell you that I've been to Vassar, but he never got a chance to meet you. Unfortunately, he died last year. But I did go back to Vassar once to drive around the campus as an adult with my children. I wish you luck, and I'm glad you had a better experience than I did."

Once I did get to Vassar, I did find out that yes, Anita Hemmings had gone there in 1893, and it's true that on her application she listed her ancestors as English and French. Her college roommate's father wondered all those years what race she was and went to Boston to find out. He found that her family lived in a black community in Boston. Her father had a shoe store. The roommate's father came back to Vassar and the week before graduation in 1897, he told the president. The board of trustees met and debated whether they would give her the degree. They did give it to her, and she was allowed to graduate with the class. She eventually married a man who went to historically black Meharry Medical College in Tennessee. He was a doctor, and they started on the West Side of New York, moved to the East Side, and vanished into the white community. Their daughter went to Vassar some twenty-five years later, as English and French, and she finished in 1927. Toward the end of her time, it was brought up to President MacCracken that this is the daughter of Anita Hemmings. He wrote back a note that said, "I don't think she even knows of her ancestry."

Civil Rights on the Campus

All of this material I found in the Vassar library. I was doing a lot of research because I was presenting this paper at the AAAVC, the Association of African American Alumni of Vassar College, a group that started in the late sixties after more blacks went to Vassar. A later alumna and I would meet with the administration, with faculty, with students, white and black, and try and get them to listen to each other—and realize that times are changing.

Eventually in the sixties, black kids occupied the main building and said they weren't going to let anybody else in except this group of black students until demands were met for an Africana Studies department, more black faculty, more black students, more black administrators. The president, Alan Simpson, came over to talk and meet with them. They ended their occupation of this building and left the building spotless. It was great. In that aftermath, the next step was trying to see how to move ahead.

This was civil rights on a college campus in the sixties. The aftermath of that kind of effort is: How do you make the next step? How do you begin to build? If you want an Africana Studies department, do people have membership in other departments as well, or should Africana Studies have enough validity on its own to exist? I think Africana Studies should be as valid as European or Latin studies.

Some think that the "real" academic departments are the old tried and true ones, not these new interdisciplinary ones.

At Vassar, when I lived at the co-op, we got ready to have one of the early parties, and I invited a boy who I met through Betty McCleary, the other black girl. He became a doctor in New York. I went to get a room for him. The people in the neighborhood around Vassar would rent rooms to students. The first two that I went to said no. The third one I went to, that person said no too. So I asked one of the white girls from the house to rent one for me.

Because I was interested in doing something, helping, I later became a Vassar trustee and served three terms. I chaired the Minority Affairs Committee, which they hadn't had before, and I pushed for increasing the number of black faculty not just in Africana Studies, but in various departments and the administration as well.

Fighting for the Rights of Japanese American Students Displaced by Relocation

I was the only black and a leader in a group of students (all white) who went to Vassar president Henry Noble MacCracken and asked if there could be scholarships for Japanese American students who had been displaced from their homes and no longer were in college. He said, "No, we couldn't possibly do that. That would be racist, just having scholarships for ethnic groups or one nationality." This incident reminds me of how black people have setbacks but don't give up. We were discouraged, but we went back to the dorm and thought about it. Then it occurred to me—I said, "Look, why don't we ask to set up some scholarships for any girls who have been in college but who have been displaced from college by virtue of being sent to relocation centers. Don't mention Japanese American or ethnicity or anything like that." So we wrote it up again and went back. The president said, "Well, yes, you're right, we can do that." Japanese Americans were the only ones, you know. German Americans were not sent off to relocation centers. It was only Japanese Americans.

A number of scholarships were set up, and maybe eight or ten girls came over the next couple of years, some came into my dorm. It was, for us, an early civil rights effort. We learned, "If you can't go at it straight, deal with the situation the way it is." You may have to go around the corner and figure out how to deal with it in a different way.

Circles That Are Close and Intertwined: Another Coincidence with the Hemmings Legacy

Like my friend Peggy, I married a man from the South, Walter Christmas. Born in North Carolina, he had grown up in New York. I met him when we were both involved in political and social action. I was in the midst of trying to get a tuberculosis hospital in Harlem for black people. This is in the fifties. Because of my work in the hospital, we went on our delayed honeymoon a year after we got married. We went to Martha's Vineyard and stayed in the house of a friend of my father's from his high school years. After a number of visits, I was talking to the woman who owned the house, and she said, "Oh, June, you know, this was Anita Hemmings's mother's house." I was incredulous. She said. "Yes, you must know about her because she went to Vassar." She explained that Anita's mother had this as a boardinghouse. After Anita finished Vassar, she would come to Martha's Vineyard, and she would stay at one of the big hotels down on Circuit Avenue. She would come over here to see her mother, but her mother would never go to see her because Anita and her husband were passing. That shows you how these circles are close and intertwined. All those years we had gone there, my parents had stayed there, and I didn't know that that had been the home of Anita Hemmings's mother where she visited after she completely passed over.

Summer Employment at Raytheon Labs

One summer at Vassar we went to Cambridge to work at Raytheon Labs. The war is on now. I went to college from '41 through '44. Class of '45. Raytheon had been known in Waltham, Massachusetts, as a place that never employed Negroes. I heard from my friends at Vassar that Raytheon was hiring college students for a special activity, and whatever they would do would be higher level than assembly-line work. I went with several other students, and a couple in front of me got sent into the college track. There were cubicles. I heard what they were saying to the other folks. When they got to me, they were talking about doing something different. I said, "Well, we are all in the same school." "No," they said, "we're sorry." They didn't have any more places, or something like that. I insisted, "No, you called for college students, and I responded." Eventually, I did get put in with the college team.

Perhaps this protest didn't matter much because I wasn't changing the system. "All right, you got in because you are a college student, but we don't want you at the next level." The institutionalized racism of a big corporate manufacturer like that remained. So the fact that they let me in with the college team did not have an impact on their institutionalized racism against black people generally.

Seeking Summer Housing in New York

During another summer break I decided to work in New York and sought housing. Half a dozen of us went to rent a place. We had enough sense not to have me go with them. The other girls rented the apartment on 8th Street right across from where the Whitney

Museum used to be, down in the Village. There were six or seven of us in three or four bedrooms. I couldn't have been there more than two weeks before somebody found out and I had to move. I wasn't on the lease. The owners had said very openly that they didn't want coloreds to stay there. So that summer, I moved in with a cousin of mine who lived in Washington Heights, off Broadway and 150th. I noticed the difference between the apartments. Her apartment was nice and big, but it was old and not that well kept up by the building owners. The apartment my friends were living in down on 8th Street was maybe not as big, but very well maintained.

Blacks at Vassar

I graduated from Vassar in December of 1944. During my time at Vassar, there was either one other black girl in any class I took or none. It was an intellectually stimulating atmosphere. One of the other things that hit me at Vassar was how few black teachers there were. Unfortunately, I can say that persisted for many years although it has changed. Students pushed to get black faculty, and eventually, after I graduated, Sterling Brown from Howard University became a visiting professor of English at Vassar. Vassar said they asked him to consider coming to Vassar as a member of the faculty, not a visiting member, but he believed he could do the best he could do by being at Howard with his permanent academic affiliation and coming as a visiting professor at Vassar.

Later, Vassar did get a black woman professor in psychology, whom I got to know as an alumna. She did not get involved in any of the social justice issues. It was the price that many black people pay. You have to do your work. You don't make waves. You work for tenure, and you stay. She was very much trying to be a model for all students.

I was willing to go out on a limb. "Toni who will say it straight." There were a couple ways that people referred to me. One of them was that. People felt that if there were issues, particularly around discrimination or injustice, that I could be counted on to tell it like it is, as the phrase went in those days. That was one thing.

But the other thing was, coming from New England. I did not speak the way some expected a black person would speak. I always spoke in modulated tones. So, I did have this other, rather pejorative nickname, which was "Lady Jackson." They said I always spoke grammatically, as if I had been to the manor born. Vivian Hall, who was a middle-class daughter of a businessman and socialist from New York, would say, "Come on, Toni, talk like a New Yorker." "But I'm not a New Yorker, Vivian." This is the way I was brought up. "To-mah-to" and "Hah-vad Yahd." Well, that's how I spoke. So there was teasing.

On the other hand, on a more serious level, if there was an issue they wanted to fight, they knew that they could get me to be part of the group, and that I could get along with people like the president, as well as some of the employees. Remember, the employees are all white. They knew that I could be counted on to stand up for all working-class people, and that I was always a lady.

Medical School

I was one of seven women in my medical school class. Seventy-six students entered in the fall of 1945, so 10 percent were women. There was one other black student there, a woman. And no black men.

I was a well-rounded student, a good student. I was involved in all kinds of activities, and I knew that I was going to be a good doctor, a well-rounded person. I wasn't somebody who thought I had to get all A's to get to medical school. I had wanted to apply to Harvard. Harvard, at that point, was not accepting women—period. Among the half dozen women accepted at Harvard Medical School a year or two later was an African American woman named Mildred Jefferson, who was the first African American woman to graduate there and later became president of the National Right to Life Committee.

In medical school, I was known as somebody who brought forth social change issues. I believed very strongly in national health insurance. I also believed we ought to increase the number of black people in medicine and the number of women in medicine, and there ought to be more opportunity for poor people to get medical care. With those views, I was soon recruited into the Association of Interns and Medical Students, a progressive organization trying to make real change in medicine, beginning with medical students. In my second or third year at Boston University, I became president of the Association of Interns and Medical Students. We tried to raise, for all the medical students, some social issues: the high cost of medical care, the importance of having health care in the neighborhood and the community, and the need for national health insurance.

We were very active in organizations. You didn't really go and do it on your own. As time went on, some of us were founders of the Medical Committee on Human Rights, activists in medicine around social issues. We were trying to make change within our communities and in society. Such persons included John Holloman, who was a physician and later the president of the Health and Hospitals Corporation in New York City. Some of us remained activists and friends over the years.

Learning from People You Serve

At Boston University, in our last years, we would go into a neighborhood and be assigned to a family. They would have a family doctor supervising us. Fortunately, I was assigned to a woman who was having a baby. I had a little experience in my obstetrics course, but not much. I remember the visiting nurse came. Finally, I think it was the mother who said it: "Don't worry, Doc, this is my eighth child, and the visiting nurse has delivered a lot of babies, right?" And the visiting nurse said, "Ninety-eight." She was a midwife. So

I figured I was probably okay. I delivered the eighth child, and realized you can always learn something from people whom you are serving, or with whom you're working. That mother obviously knew a lot more than I did. The visiting nurse knew more than I did. Being in that community was a learning experience.

Interning in New York City: The Intersection of Class and Race

When I got to New York, I interned. No real problems in medicine there. But I did notice every once in a while I would have as a patient at Queens General Hospital the mother of someone who was a well-known African American person in the theater, or that person himself. I would think, now here it is an underfunded public hospital, and this patient I would expect to be at Mount Sinai or Columbia Presbyterian. I realized that sometimes when you're sick, you're down to the fundamentals. You don't have the money, or you don't feel you'd be accepted and given good medical care because you weren't given good medical care in the past, in the South or in the North. Therefore, this is where you think you belong. I realized, too, that even if they had the money, they may not necessarily feel they'd be that welcomed at Mount Sinai or Presbyterian Hospital. We tried to give good quality care, but it was a public hospital and it was not a place that people with money would seek to go first.

Denied Work as Medical Resident Because of Fear That Negro Women Doctors Would Be Sexually Stimulating to White Patients

I had met, through my friend Peggy Miller, Benjamin Miller, who wrote books on the practice of medicine. He was a middle-aged Euro-American who had published popular books. He also urged

Peggy and me to continue to write our book. He arranged an interview for me at New York Hospital's psychiatric division.

Dr. Oskar Diethelm, head of Payne Whitney Hospital, interviewed me. After the interview, he said, "Dr. Jackson, I could never have you here as a resident because you're a Negro woman, and a Negro woman would be sexually stimulating to the white patients. The men would be very disturbed at you and stimulated by you, and it just wouldn't work." I was twenty-five years old, trying to explain to this very authoritarian man with a German Prussian accent why that would not necessarily be so, and that I can behave professionally and the patient would be a patient and I would try to understand any behavior the patient had, just as with any other symptoms. He said, "No. You would be a very good addition, except for the fact that you're a Negro woman."

Attempting to Create a TB Hospital in Harlem

In the fifties, I was doing my residency at Bellevue. An interracial group of us started pushing to start a tuberculosis hospital in Harlem. Everybody else was saying, "No more hospitals. We've got these wonder drugs like streptomycin." But because black people living in overcrowded situations were very likely to become infected and to reinfect people in the family, they still may need sanitaria. I began working with this group, meeting at night in an office in Midtown Manhattan and at the Committee for the Arts, Sciences, and Professionals, which was a left-wing organization.

There was a very good-looking man who was at the desk. He was the office manager, and he had the most beautiful voice I ever heard. I would be looking at him until finally somebody said to me, "Do you know Walter Christmas?" No, I didn't. So he introduced me and one other member of the group, Dorothy Crichlow. Dorothy said, "He's a friend of my husband's, that's how we happen to have this space here." Her husband was Ernest Crichlow, a painter. So I found some reason to use the phone. Walter and I finally met, and we began going out. We never did get the TB hospital, but I got a husband.

Leading Change

Many years later I discovered that the Psychiatric Institute at Columbia, which rarely had black patients back in the forties and fifties, was a state hospital but exclusively selected their patients. Because they were a research hospital, they were able to keep people out. No blacks. No average working-class people. When I became mental health commissioner, one of my efforts was to get the state psychiatric hospital system to work in a more coordinated way with the city hospital system and the not-for-profits like Columbia Presbyterian and New York Hospital. One of the reasons I ended up as mental health commissioner is that I was at Harlem Hospital, and one of the reasons I was in Harlem Hospital is that when Harlem Hospital became affiliated with Columbia in the early sixties, Elizabeth Davis reached out to me. She, too, was a psychiatrist, an African American, whose father had been the rector of St. Philip's Church. Beth realized Harlem needed more than a clinic and began to build a department of psychiatry based on a small clinic there.

Earlier, a wonderful old man named Dr. Harold Ellis, one of the earliest black psychiatrists in New York City, had started a small outpatient clinic affiliated with Harlem Hospital. He was from Saint Kitts. Harold Ellis formed this little clinic and struggled to keep it alive. Harlem Hospital itself had been slow to hire black doctors in the twenties and thirties.

Modifying My Views on Psychoanalysis

Now, one of the reasons that I began to consider modifying my view as to the importance of psychoanalysis was that I'd run into a little bit of a stumbling block during my training at Bellevue. I went to Bellevue for my residency after my internship at Queens. I was making fifty dollars a month. In the second year, I had the opportunity to make more by applying for a Veterans Administration residency. I applied for that and got it. That meant I was technically at Bellevue, but I would spend my days over at the VA clinic in lower Manhattan.

I was there for maybe two or three months when all of a sudden I got a thick letter. Something to do with the FBI, it said there was a question of my loyalty oath. At that point, everybody was supposed to sign a loyalty oath, and I remember thinking, "Oh, well, am I going to or am I not going to sign?" The letter went beyond the loyalty oath, because it alleged "proof" that the federal government had information that I was not a loyal citizen. What they had found goes back to my civil rights involvement in my medical school days. I had marched with groups for the rights of black people. Those groups included communists. During high school, I had corresponded with a student in Czechoslovakia. And I had attended interracial parties. My boyfriend in medical school was white, and we had attended interracial gatherings. Well, it went through this long list and it said that, therefore, I was not eligible. I had been an activist, an agitator for change.

I went to see a civil rights lawyer in New York, a progressive lawyer, and began talking about what I had done. There had been many cases of lynchings back in the thirties and forties, and I had marched with people and other groups against lynching, the poll tax, and racial segregation and discrimination. In addition to organizations like the Catholic Church, the Presbyterian Church, Reform Jews, the NAACP, the Urban League, there would be the Communist Party—there would be all kinds of groups. So my answer was, "Yes, I did march with communists. There were Catholics, there were nuns, there were this group and that and the other." But my answer toward the end was that all of these things that I was doing were to make change, to support the Fair Employment Practices Commission that A. Philip Randolph was trying to start, to bring an end to racist acts. In college, I wrote essays in the college newspaper saying that it was too bad that when Roosevelt did set up the FEPC it only applied to the military and the war effort but didn't apply generally. Yes, I had been an activist. I'd been working for the best of America. In the end they agreed with me and stated in a letter that I am a loyal citizen of the United States.

Fighting Housing Discrimination

Walter had been very active politically on the left. I had been active, but maybe not as left as he was. I had been more in mixed groups mainly, liberal church groups, interracial relations committees. This became an area we worked on together. When we married, I was still at Bellevue, and I said, "We've got to find a place to live."

One of the biggest things I believe in civil rights is the right to have a place to live—in addition to education and health—housing. I had a little one-room apartment down on East 2nd Street, and I had got it through the newspaper in '51 or '52. I had called, and the man—he was Russian and an artist—said, "Yes, it's available. Come and look at it." When he saw me, the man's face dropped. He said, "Well, I really didn't expect to see somebody—so young." He did rent to me with a sublease. When Walter and I got married, we moved into this little apartment. There was at Bellevue with me a woman psychiatrist who said to me, "Oh, where are you two living?" We're starting off at my apartment because Walter's apartment on the Lower East Side was even smaller than this one. By that point, he was working for the Youth Board, which was a community social action group for young people. Anyway, Alex Symonds said, "Why don't you folks take over our apartment?" And we said, "Take over your apartment?" He said, "We're buying a house in Brooklyn Heights and we have six or seven months left on the one lease and we have the right to sublease." We said, "Okay."

They spoke to their landlord and the landlord said, "Dr. Symonds, any friend of yours is a friend of mine." They said, "Dr. Christmas is a colleague of ours." They brought the papers for Walter and me to sign, which we did. This was by now about '53 or so. They moved out on a particular Saturday and we were all ready to move in. Now, we knew that we might have a problem because housing was certainly not open in New York City. We moved in, and by the end of that Saturday, the landlord called Dr. Symonds and said, "Dr. Symonds what did you do to me?" "What do you mean, what did you do to me?" "They're Negroes." "I know they're Negroes." So, he said, "I don't know what I'm going to do." So he ranted and raved for a while, and then he said, "I don't know what we're going to do." We moved in and after the three or four months, the lease was due to be up. I knew, according to what we had signed, we were supposed to get another one-year lease. We stayed there for most of the next year, and we had maybe a couple of months more to go when I became pregnant and we said, "Well, we really need to look for a larger place." I wanted to look for something in Manhattan because by then I was working at various clinics. We began looking in Manhattan, and when we found a place, we called the landlord, whom we'd spoken to a couple of times. "Do you want us to find somebody to take over the rest of the lease?" "Oh, no, Dr. Christmas, don't worry. That's perfectly all right. You don't have to find anybody."

This was only one of our encounters with housing discrimination in New York. After we moved, and began looking for our next apartment, I began looking both for a place to rent for my office and for a place for us to live. This is by now 1954 going into '55. Our son Vincent was born in '55. I would call, and the first thing that anybody responding would say was, "No blacks or Puerto Ricans." Because of the way I talked, I was not presumed to be black. Sometimes I would let them go on and talk about how there were no

blacks or Puerto Ricans. If it was a place that didn't sound interesting, I would say, "That's too bad, because I am black." "Oh, oh,
oh." I must have gone through almost a couple of hundred places,
making calls, and I would say maybe a third of them—at least, or
half—would have some variation of, "Don't worry, there will be no
blacks or Puerto Ricans here."

We finally did get to a place at 200 West 90th where a woman
realtor had a somewhat different action. Her response was, "Oh,
you'd love this building. Paul Robeson thought he was going to
move here, but he moved to our other building." We gradually came
to realize that in Manhattan in the 1950s there were two buildings,
1200 Fifth Avenue and 200 West 90th Street, that were the first
two buildings on the Upper East Side and Upper West Side to rent
to Negroes. They were both upper-middle-class real estate, owned
by the same company. We rented 200 West 90th Street, a classic
six-room apartment. I don't know whether this story is apocryphal
or not, but we were told that the buildings had been owned by brothers who fell to fighting over something. One of them said, "Well,
all right, I'll rent to Negroes," and that's how they began to rent to
Negroes at 200 West 90th. By the time we moved in, it was quite
integrated, maybe 60 percent white, 40 percent black. No Latinos.
The one on Fifth Avenue had fewer blacks, but they were of a higher
income—Paul Robeson, Juanita Hall, and a few others like that.

Our family soon had three children under six. We were looking
for a large apartment where I could have my private practice of psychiatry and psychoanalysis. One day, walking down 94th Street,
I saw a couple of run-down-looking buildings, brownstones. I
thought, "Isn't that just like white people. They think we would live
anywhere." I got home and I said to Walter, "Can you imagine somebody from the park suggested we ought to think about one of those
buildings on 94th Street?" Ninety-fourth Street had a lot of people
sitting on the stoops, a lot of run-down-looking buildings, and it
was a mess. So Walter said, "Well, did you look at the buildings?"

I said I could barely look at them. He said, "Maybe the neighbor-hood is changing, and the building might have some potential." I thought, "Oh my goodness. That's Walter, such an optimist." So the next time we looked, maybe there weren't so many people sitting on the stoop.

On the phone, the owner said, "Dr. Christmas, the view from that apartment would be therapeutic to your patients. Why don't you and your husband come down and sign tomorrow morning?" That would have been Friday. We said we were going away for the weekend. He said, "I'd like to get it settled before the weekend." He urged us to grab the apartment, an elegant, large eight-room dwelling where I could practice. So we went down to his office in Midtown, where we had a ten o'clock appointment to sign the lease. We sat and we sat and we sat. Finally, after about thirty or forty minutes or so, Walter said, "We have a ten o'clock appointment." "Oh, yeah, just a moment, just a moment." Finally the owner said, "We just decided that we are not going to rent that apartment." "You decided not to rent the apartment? But you told us at six o'clock last night to come here first thing in the morning." "Yes, well, I decided I'm going to move into it myself." Walter was having none of that. So he said, "What is this?" "Oh, Mr. Christmas, don't think it's dis-crimination. It's not because you're Negroes, no, no, not at all." He went through some long explanation about how he was German, he had seen what Nazis had done, he was a Jew, he could under-stand. No, no, he wouldn't be discriminating at all. All of a sudden he was thinking the night before that he really ought to move into the city and that's what he should do. And he went on and on with some elaborate story. Walter told him he didn't believe him. "This is something you concocted when you saw that we were Negroes." I was pretty quiet.

We then went to the Fair Housing Board. In New York in the fifties, it took maybe a year and a half for this ever to be heard. By then, the Strykers had literally moved into their apartment. At the hearing, Mr. Stryker's defense was that he didn't want psychiatric patients there. So when they got to me and queried me, I said, "He told me, 'Dr. Christmas, the view from this apartment would be therapeutic for your patients.'" He gasped a bit. He said, "I told Dr. Christmas that we did not want to rent to *Negroes*, I mean psychiatrists." So, Freud was sitting in the room at that point. We won the case. Our bringing that suit actually led to a permanent change in the housing laws in New York City.

The 94th Street Town House

Walter looked at it and saw it might have some possibilities. We decided to take a chance, especially since no apartment was renting to us, big or small. We bought the house in 1960, renovated it, and moved in 1961. We also had a couple of guest rooms, so we began having in our guest rooms some of the young folks who were down in the South, in the field, risking their lives working in civil rights activities. Voter people from SNCC and with SCLC, and others working on independence movements in Africa.

We met a lot of the young folks, H. Rap Brown and Stokely Carmichael, all those folks had either stayed or been at our home. We had fundraisers. Walter was in public relations, and I was working at that point in private practice. We used our home both for raising money for the Civil Rights Movement and as a place for people to come and stay when they were in New York. And people always wanted to come to New York because they were battle-weary.

I worked then at Harlem doing group therapy and discovered that some of the parents were very capable of fighting the system. They can go in there and argue with teachers, and maybe have a controlled argument with the principal, but with their kids, they lost control. I was trying to help parents take their strengths and build them into something that could be good for them with their families but not destructive in the school system. From that, I began to model training programs and using paraprofessionals—people who aren't professionally trained, who have innate ability and whom you can train to play a role as a bridge, or an advocate, or as somebody just supporting whatever work you as a professional are doing. I developed that program at Harlem Hospital.

During the second and third year I was there, people asked me if I didn't want to go south. I talked to Walter, and I said, "I'm scared to death to go to the South." The furthest south I'd been is Washington, D.C., as an exchange student from Vassar for a long weekend.

Then I said, "Why not?" It was 1964. I went south, asked to go by SNCC. The SNCC workers had been coming up to our house for a couple of years, and so they said, "We come back from the field— we're exhausted. We need some counseling sessions, individual and group, to help figure out how to recoup our energy."

We went to Atlanta, and those students came in from the field, and I must say, I was so impressed with them. John Lewis, Diane Nash, Matthew Jones, all of them. They were people who you knew had inner strength and abilities. At different points, Walter worked with the government of Ghana and with Martin Luther King as director of the foundation to which he directed his Nobel Peace Prize award.

My Professional Life

The Health and Hospitals Corporation was the organization that brought all the public hospitals together. It was their overall governing body. It hadn't been in existence for many years, but in those years it had seemed as though its presidents were all traditional physicians, not necessarily people who really believed in seeing what people needed, but imposing what they thought was needed.

John L. S. Holloman, called Mike, was the first black president of the Health and Hospitals Corporation of New York City. He was a founder of the Medical Committee on Human Rights and had been in the military. In the early seventies, it occurred to a number of us that Mike Holloman would be the person to be president of the Health and Hospitals Corporation. The corporation was always underfunded by New York City. Those of us working in various community hospitals realized that having a black president there was just part of change. It was not enough unless you had funding and a commitment from the mayor and from a board that is really going to back up the kind of change that this person wants to bring about. This would be more ambulatory clinics—putting community health services where they are needed, not just where they have been traditionally. Make change, but for the better.

I had been appointed commissioner of mental health for the City of New York by Mayor Lindsay in '72 and reappointed by Mayor Beame. Once I got to be the mental health commissioner of the city, it was expected that I should have been responsible only to the mayor. That's a dutiful soldier. You pay attention to the person who appointed you. But I also believed that I had a conscience and that if there were support for programs and services behind Mike Holloman, he would be more successful. But in a year or two, Mayor Beame said, "No, he's got to go." Many of us were very upset. Since I sat on the board by virtue of being the mental health commissioner, I know what I'm supposed to do. The mayor called me in and said, "June, we are going to take a vote, and I expect to get rid of him." I said, "Now remember, Mayor Beame, I believe that he needs to have more opportunity and more resources." I tried to persuade the mayor. Well, he said, "No, you know, you do what's right." And I said, "Well, I have to do what's right, yes." So, when it came time to vote, I voted my conscience and voted not to get rid of him. I can't say my vote didn't count, it counted, but the point is the mayor had the majority of the votes on the board. Anyway, I remember his coming over and saying, "June, what happened?" And I said, "Mayor Beame, I did say to you that I felt I had to vote my conscience on that." He said, "Well, all right, if you did, you did."

Boston University was taking pictures of alums to be on the wall of the medical school. When they asked me what I would say about myself, it took a while for me to figure that out. I was trying to encapsulate what I thought that medical school experience had contributed to my ongoing activism as well as trying to deliver quality care. I said only as much as you can put on a three-by-five card.

It said in part, "June Jackson Christmas, MD, Boston University School of Medicine, 1949. Medical Professor Emeritus of Behavioral Medicine, School of Bio-Medical Education, City University of New York." That was that particular title; I didn't put my Columbia title. What I said about me was: lifelong commitment to community health began as a medical student working with families in home health care; founded Harlem Rehabilitation Center (that's later in the sixties); pioneered in hiring and training local residents as psychosocial mental health workers. Under three mayors, served as commissioner of Mental Health, Mental Retardation and Alcoholism Services of New York City.

Recent photo of Dr. June Jackson Christmas. (Credit: Gordon Christmas)

Aileen Clarke Hernandez in the civil rights era. (Credit: Joe Rosenthal / San Francisco Chronicle / Polaris)

3

AILEEN HERNANDEZ

Aileen Hernandez began her activism as a student leader at Howard University during the 1940s. In then legally segregated Washington, D.C., Hernandez experienced firsthand the effects of racism and also witnessed the impact of war on both her educational opportunities and opportunities to take on greater roles in the larger society.

She became the first woman and first African American to be appointed to the Equal Employment Opportunity Commission (EEOC) in 1964. She was the first African American president of the National Organization for Women. Hernandez resigned from the EEOC because of its unwillingness to address sexual harassment; she left NOW when it elected an all-white officer slate. Hernandez co-founded the National Women's Political Caucus and Black Women Organized for Political Action.

She was a pioneer in addressing issues concerning the intersectionality of race, sex, and class. She was socially active her entire life, until shortly before she died at age ninety in 2017. At the time of our interview in 2013, she was on the board of the San Francisco Human Rights Commission. Modest and unassuming, she still took the bus to the commission meetings and her various other activities.

The Black Taxi

I grew up in the northern part of the country. When my parents immigrated from Jamaica, they came to Harlem in New York City. The Jamaicans who moved to New York came together in Harlem, so they had all kinds of activities—theatrical events, music, and all the rest. It was the era of all the marvelous literature and music coming out of Harlem. But it was getting really crowded, really a problem. My mother and father decided that they could not live up there with three children, and they needed to find a place that was less hard. We moved from Harlem to a neighborhood in Brooklyn. We were the only black family on our street. In Brooklyn, my father and my mother both were involved with the NAACP. Having come from Jamaica, which was quite different from the United States, they could not adjust to the idea of all this segregation. It was not what they had learned in Jamaica. My father and my mother believed in challenging discrimination. Whenever they went to meetings, my two brothers and I would sit in chairs out in the hallway. We were given books to read while my mother and father went inside and heard all about what was going on and what they could do. I had good parents. They expected us to do some things, that was for sure.

I would say that the Civil Rights Movement really got me involved in all the things that I did after I became aware of what was going on in the United States. Because I wasn't always aware. I really started late in the Civil Rights Movement. I didn't think there was a problem in New York. I thought New York was a great city, and no problems were going on there. It was going to Howard University in Washington, D.C., that started me. I was so struck by the capital of the United States with all of the segregation and all the rest of it. I could not believe that a country that really believed itself to be a democracy was that way.

I had won a scholarship from my public all-girls high school in

Brooklyn. It was a great school, a marvelous place. They opened up all kinds of opportunities for girls that you didn't get in those days. I had great teachers, and I loved being there. I graduated from high school in 1943, and when I got the scholarship, my mother and father thought: yes, we would love to have you go to Howard University. My father took me down on the train.

On the train, I got hungry somewhere along the line, and my father said, "Let's go get a sandwich or something in the car." So I said, "Car? We have a car that we're going to?" He said, "No, we're going to go down there. They have a place on the train where you can eat." We went, we sat down, and people came in and asked us what we wanted to eat. I noticed that everybody who came through the door was African American. They came over, and they started to smile when they saw me. When they asked me where I was going and I said Howard University, they smiled even bigger. It turned out that most of the people working on the train, who were all black men, had graduated from Howard University. They were on the train giving us food, when they had gotten all of this great education at Howard. They talked to us all the way to Washington. When we got close to Washington, they said, "We're going to get organized, now. We're going to get your trunk, and your father should take you out. There will be a taxi, and that taxi will take you up to Howard University."

Now, we're New Yorkers. We're not aware that there is total segregation in Washington, D.C. My father and I get off the train in Washington, and we do exactly what the gentlemen told us. When we get out, there is a taxi waiting. My father goes over to it. They had told him, "Look for the black taxi." My father went over looking for a black taxi, and never saw a black taxi. So he walked to the first taxi that was there. He said to the man, who was reading a magazine, that we were going up to Howard University. Could we get the taxi? The man looked up from the pages and he said to my father, "You'll have to get the black taxi." So we said, "There isn't any black taxi." We did not realize that what he was telling us was there were taxis for black people and there were taxis for people who were not black people, and we had to get a separate taxi that would go up to Howard University's campus, where I was going to be in school for the next four years.

We were struck by this. But my father got us the taxi. We did get up to Howard University. The man who had the taxi explained to us how Washington operated. And I wasn't sure that I wanted to go to Howard at that point in time. But after I was there for a while, I realized it was the best thing that ever happened to me.

Howard University

This was the 1940s, and we were at war. My older brother was in the military service while I was going through Howard, he was in the war in the Pacific in a segregated unit. Going into the military was really a change for him, because we were in a neighborhood which was really very diverse. We had everybody. We had Germans. We had Jewish people. We were the black people, one group. But we had all of these others, so we got to know people across lines in ways that we would not have if we had gone south, where we would have been in a totally black area.

At Howard, I was struck by how good the teachers were, and how much they really related to the students. They took the students into all of these meetings. They were just beginning to come up with strategies for what to do to change not only Washington but the United States as a whole, on some of the things that were supposedly within the Constitution but really weren't. All of these incredible scholars were coming into Howard University to begin what is essentially the Civil Rights Movement. The law school had a whole program going where they brought lawyers from all over the country to come in and work on an approach to take segregation issues to the courts and get a decision that would actually end them. We sat there and listened to names that are historic now, and we learned that we had a responsibility to do something about this I got more and more excited about what was going on, and about changing what I had just seen with the people and the black taxi.

I got the chance to sit in on some of the meetings that were being held by these lawyers who were talking about, "Here's the strategy, here's what we're gonna do." That was helpful to just get that, and then to be able to use it. In those days, people sent their daughters to Howard University to look for husbands much more than they thought about, "What is going to be my career?" I got there at this incredible time where all of this was changing, where people were looking at this idea differently about how women could be part of it. There were all kinds of women who were a part of the Civil Rights Movement that you might never have heard of but who did a lot of things in Washington, D.C., to be part of the changes.

We were at the forefront of changes in our society. The girls could do things that they hadn't done before, partially because the boys were gone. We had the lowest male enrollment in our school in our class, because they were all in the military. So we were left on the campus to take courses that we would probably not have taken before. I think a lot of us, particularly the girls, were opening up into areas where they had not gone before. Very few women were going into law at that stage or going into anything except being a teacher, and mostly an elementary school teacher.

There were people who were at Howard University who actually marched in the parades for women's rights in the early days of the suffragist movement. The Delta Sigma Theta and Alpha Kappa Alpha sororities at Howard marched in the first suffragist parade in Washington, D.C., in 1913. Nobody ever mentions black women marched in it in those days. In fact, most of the black women had been told that they didn't want them to be in the parade. It was going to be done mostly by white women. But the black women said, "No way. We're going to be part of this," and they marched.

What you're seeing is a very different picture from what I thought was going to happen in Washington, D.C. Howard University was a very similar environment to what I had gotten in high school, where we had all girls and were given all of these opportunities. I get down to Howard University, and I find we can do something here. Girls actually got involved. They changed their majors. They were doing things that were different from what they had come there for. They began to do a lot of work that hadn't been done before.

Pauli Murray, a good friend of mine who was at the law school at the time, was head of the Civil Rights Committee of the Howard NAACP chapter and involved with changing Washington, D.C. We were really focusing on Washington because it was the capital. It was in the South, just on the other side of the Mason-Dixon Line. As students, we could not go to certain restaurants. The only place you could go and sit down with somebody who was not black was at the Labor Department, where they had a lunch room where black and white people could go and eat sitting down together. In Washington, otherwise, no black people could go into most of the restaurants.

Our class was one of the classes that began picketing in Washington, D.C.—mostly right around Howard University. There was a little restaurant across the road where you could buy something, but we couldn't sit there and eat it. We'd have to go back to the school and eat it. If we went downtown to buy something in a department store, we could buy things, but we were not allowed to try them on. We were living in a very difficult kind of society. Our professors helped us understand that we had a responsibility to change it.

The list of people who were my teachers is remarkable. Not only for what they did in the classroom, but they invited you to their homes. For example, Sterling Brown, an incredible poet, was also a jazz lover. If you took English from Sterling Brown, he would invite you to come to his house, and he would get out his records. He would play the records and recite his poems. We saw a different kind of teacher.

I started out at Howard to become a teacher, as most girls did in those days. There was not much else you could do. I finally decided not to take that course of study. I didn't want to just be an elementary school teacher after I had heard what was going on in the campus. I changed my focus of study to public areas, particularly to political science.

I was the editor of the school newspaper at Howard University for two years. I also wrote articles elsewhere about what we were finding in Washington, D.C. The newspaper that was willing to take my articles wanted to know what was going on at Howard, so I was able to do some work with them. So I started from that, and I got more and more involved as I went along.

I graduated from Howard in 1947 with a degree in political science and sociology. At that point, I had to decide what I wanted to do. Since I was in everything, I wore myself out and I got sick. I went back home to Brooklyn and decided, after I was feeling better, that I should go on and get a master's degree at New York University. So I did that.

The International Ladies' Garment Workers' Union

I remember sitting in the NYU library working on a paper, and I got tired because it was kind of boring. I said, I think I'll take a little rest. Maybe I'll just read a magazine or something. There was a magazine on the table. So I got up, got this magazine, brought it back, and started reading. There was an ad in the magazine, and what the ad said was: "Are you an oddball? Would you like a job that doesn't pay you very much money but gives you an opportunity to be involved in some very interesting things?" I said, "They're talking to me!" At the end of the ad, there was a telephone number, and it said, "Please call." So I called. It turned out to be the International Ladies' Garment Workers' Union, the ILGWU, which I knew about because a lot of black women were employed in the shops that made all the clothing for women.

I called one of my friends from the International Ladies' Garment Workers' Union, and I asked him what it was all about. I had also gotten deeply involved with the Democratic Party, and with some changes that they were in the midst of doing, so I knew a number of men also involved in political activities. He said, "Well, our president decided that we need some new, young people coming into the union. So he set up this program, which is a one-year program. If you go through the one year and you come out okay, you can get a job at the other end of it. You could go work anywhere the ILGWU is active." I said, "Oh, that sounds pretty good."

I was one of four women who were selected. In spite of the fact that it was the International Ladies' Garment Workers' Union, of the thirty-two people who were selected to come into this training program, twenty-eight were men and four were women. So we knew right away that just because "women" is in the title doesn't mean that women are really in power in the organization. It was a great program. We had excellent people who came in and not only taught us what goes on in the garment factory; they also talked to us about philosophies and the importance of politics, because politics changes laws and does all of these things. So this is something you can really have an impact on.

The very first day I came for that program, I met Eleanor Roosevelt. She came to talk to this group of people who were selected. When I met Mrs. Roosevelt, I was delighted, because I used to wave at her in Brooklyn when her husband was the governor of the State of New York. He used to come through our neighborhoods periodically, and all of the kids who were in the elementary schools could come down and wave at him as the car went by. So I had been waving at Mr. and Mrs. Roosevelt for four years of my childhood. I was delighted to have a chance to talk to her and really enjoyed what she had to say. She was a remarkable woman. Eleanor Roosevelt was involved with the unions because she believed very strongly in the importance of labor issues. In fact, she had persuaded her husband to bring in a woman, Frances Perkins, as the first commissioner of the New York State Department of Labor. When the governor became the president, he brought Perkins down to Washington, and she became the secretary of labor for the United States as a whole. So we immediately got to meet somebody who was actually working on unions and who was a woman. So that opened doors, and just kept opening up possibilities for me.

I graduated from that training program in 1950. When they asked me where I wanted to go to work, I said California. Now, that sounds like something a really young person says: "I live in New York. I'm tired of living in New York. I want to go as far away as I can possibly go. I'll go to California." I went to Los Angeles and started out as an organizer for the International Ladies' Garment Workers' Union. I was with the union for over eleven years. Over the years, I became the director of education and public relations for the West Coast region. We trained a lot of people. We had a lot of immigrants that came into the ILGWU. We trained them on how to become citizens. We trained them in the English language. We had a huge amount of things that we could work on. It was excellent for looking at the whole world and looking at what was happening in the United States as a whole.

The ILGWU was deeply involved in politics. I had opportunities to connect with other people who were involved in politics and opening up the union arrangements so there would be more unions to give people better working conditions. As the labor unions grew, more people began looking at working-class people—what was happening with them, and what was good and what was not good for them.

Beyond just being involved with the people who were in the International Ladies' Garment Workers' Union, the ILG also joined the big organizations of all the labor unions coming together. So as a result of that, I got to meet all of the people who were running the American Federation of Labor (AFL) and the Congress of Industrial Organizations (CIO). The unions got together, along with some of the community-based people, to figure out how to get some laws passed in California that would improve the labor situation and make it possible to get changes in how much people earned in the various industries that we were talking about. Health issues were also a focus for the ILG, because the shops in which most of the women and the men worked were not very nice. There was a lot of dust in them. They were usually in very small places which were not well ventilated. They just didn't work right in those days because they didn't care.

Garment industry workers certainly needed help, so they began to get laws passed. In 1945, you got a Fair Employment Practice Commission in New York State, the first one in the country. The commission said the government has the right to get in here and improve the way in which these unions operate, and the way in which these industries operate, for a better life for people who were living and working in the shops. There were a large number of women working in the shops, and a lot of those industries in the ILGWU were in the New York area.

When I came to California, because New York had passed a fair employment practice law, California began to organize to get one passed. We brought people from all kinds of areas, not just the unions. People who were concerned about health and people who were concerned about education came together so that they actually pushed the State of California to pass a fair employment practice law in 1959.

The ILG opened up a lot of opportunities for me. I was lucky. I got to meet a lot of people that I would never have met otherwise. And I began to have a philosophy about what I thought I wanted to do for the rest of my life, which was essentially to go out and try to make changes. I believed very strongly that the United States was not a democracy at that point in time. We had almost no people in Congress who were people of non-white backgrounds, for example. Almost none. Certainly no women were around. So we had a lot of work to do to get me in, because I represented both of those groups. I'm a woman who is a person of color. If I was going to satisfy myself that I was doing something useful, then I would have to be involved and deal with all of these issues. I'd have to get to know people better who were involved in all of these things that I was talking about.

When I left the ILGWU, for about a year I traveled through six countries in Latin America. The State Department had given me an opportunity to come and talk about unions and what was happening in the international areas. After that, I got a call from the governor's office in California asking me if I would be interested in being on the staff of the first Fair Employment Practice Commission in California. So I came up to San Francisco from Los Angeles to be the second person on the staff of the California Fair Employment Practice Commission. I worked there as assistant chief starting in November of 1962.

When we finally passed a fair employment law on the national level as Title VII of the Civil Rights Act of 1964, I was asked to come and work as commissioner for the Equal Employment Opportunity Commission created by that law starting in May of 1965. We had just passed a law that said women also needed to be put into these areas where they could change what they were doing in life and do the things that they were capable of doing even if people thought women ought not to be doing them. It's the very first law that had ever been passed on a national level involving women. Most of the other laws talk only about race—they didn't talk about women at that stage.

Now, the problem we had on the national level was that the EEOC had very little money, very little staff, and very little power. The first law that was passed on creating the EEOC was a very un-useful law because we had no opportunity to do anything if we found discrimination except to go and talk to people. It wasn't until the Equal Employment Opportunity Act of 1972 that they added to the law so that there was more power.

National Organization for Women

I was invited to speak as representative of the EEOC at the Third National Conference of Commissions on the Status of Women in June of 1966. The women who came to that conference came from every part of the United States. It was amazing. You would not have had that many women from all of these states if it had not been for the initial Presidential Commission on the Status of Women that John Kennedy created and Mrs. Roosevelt was the head of. In fact, Pauli Murray, my close friend from Howard, had worked with Mrs. Roosevelt on the initial Presidential Commission. She was on her committee doing staff work and lawyer's work, and we talked periodically.

At the Third National Conference of Commissions on the Status of Women, they were saying, "We now have this new law, and it talks about women. So what are we gonna do?" I said, "We don't have any power. We don't really have much staff. We need to get some help to make this law more effective for women to be able to change this, and for all the racial and ethnic groups that also came under the law."

The National Organization for Women, NOW, was founded at that conference. A woman by the name of Betty Friedan had written a book, and she was there to talk about it. She wanted to read from her book about what was going on, and she also wanted to figure out how that new law might be changing some of the things that she was complaining about. She decided, with some of the women sitting at her lunch table, that maybe they should spend a little more time talking about this. So they invited some women up to her hotel room for the evening to figure out: How do we make this work better for women? Among them was Pauli Murray.

Pauli was a lawyer, and she was saying the law has no power. A lot of the young women lawyers were saying, "This law has no power, so we can't do anything. We have to change it. We need to get people organized." So we're back to organizing again, and we're getting people back into it. Pauli came up with a lot of the ideas about what changes needed to be made in the law. So here I keep getting people who were coming out of my old days at Howard University showing up again in another part of my life. She said, "You're here now, Aileen, we ought to talk about this."

Pauli was one of the people at Howard who had us out there picketing and demonstrating and doing all the rest of it. She said very often, "You have to show that you have some power. You have to bring people together, and you have to be out there in the communities so that people understand what you're trying to do with the laws that you're talking about. Otherwise, things are not gonna change." We ran into each other at a lot of meetings as we went along. So we kept connecting again. We didn't know this was gonna happen. We hadn't planned it. But we kept finding ourselves in the same places. So Pauli and a number of other people I knew were part of the group of people that started saying, "We need to do something."

Because NOW was founded at this conference that involved women who had been selected to be on Mrs. Roosevelt's committee, there was a strange mix of people that you would never have had before. If you're getting appointed to a committee that's in Washington, D.C., and the president of the committee is Mrs. Roosevelt, you've got some real power. You're going to get everybody. This is an important committee to be on. That committee did not have a lot of women of color on it. From all over the country they were coming, but most of them were not women of color. We had a good handful of women of color, like Pauli, and some who had been involved in the NAACP and the like, who were lawyers and were looking at this from the point of view of law and saw the connection between what we were doing on "general" civil rights and what we had not begun to do on women. They saw that they needed to come together for more power, and that they needed to understand that it was really bigger than any of the things that they were doing individually.

People were coming from all the different states in the country at that stage to that conference. They heard the same kinds of things. It was interesting to me, as I saw NOW coming into play. I talked to a lot of these people.

Most of the people who were at that conference had been from New York. So they could pick up where they left off that first day after listening to me speak, deciding that something needed to be done, and having Pauli Murray there to talk about what might be done, and go with that. Once we got back home, it was much harder to organize in the West than it was in New York. I acted as western regional vice president for about three years with NOW. We had a national thing that we would never have been able to put together otherwise. Four months later, I gave notice to the Equal Employment Opportunity Commission because I thought it didn't have much to do, and decided to come back and continue my education to see what I wanted to do. The unions were very active on civil rights issues. We had committees working on those issues in California, and many of the people that were on those committees were from all of the unions. So they had pushed for fair housing laws, for fair employment laws, now here's the women's law so they're there again. We had a large group of people who were ready to move. A huge group. One third of the country is union when we're talking at that stage of the game. We began to see connections. People actually got involved in unions who had never been involved before. People who were in unions also got involved with women's issues, which they had never addressed to any great degree before.

I was the second national president of NOW from March 1970 to

September 1971. What was very important to me was that we had a number of black women who were on those committees. I knew that I was gonna have to do some more work in getting women of color. Because I was not about to do something that didn't understand that this was not just women; it was about civil rights across the board for everybody. Women needed to be part of a bigger group in order to make the changes that were necessary.

Pauli worked with other women lawyers to figure out what are the strategies to do things for this issue. They realized that we needed to organize across the entire United States. It can't just be in one area, and we need to get all kinds of people to be there. We need all kinds of women. We had great women who were black in the beginning. But they were only there for a short period of time because they were already working in other places. As NOW grew, we began to see fewer and fewer women of color coming into NOW.

This is a huge group of people. If you're doing something with all the women of the United States, that's a lot of people. So it had to come together, is what we were saying. We had to say to those women, as we began to look at the issues that we were gonna deal with, the feminist issues, that you have to broaden those issues. You had to look at where women were, what they were doing, and what you needed to do to move to the next level. We were lucky, because we did find a way of connecting. And we did it because we had some people who were in politics at that point in time who were not necessarily the friends of any of us.

We did a lot of things. But then when we got some other people coming in, some of them had never been involved in anything like this, any kind of politics, any kind of civic interest. They were learning for the first time. It was a sort of power situation with them, and they wanted the groups that they could work with closest. I didn't think that's what you should do. So I said to the NOW people, "This is not what we should be doing. We are not here just to get our own groups moving forward. We're here to make a change in the society as a whole, and I think we have to do that." I said it publicly. I didn't go without saying it publicly, because I knew it had to be said publicly. That women could not think this was somehow just for some women who had the right to get in there and argue this question. This was about a huge issue that had never been addressed before.

Cultivating Leadership

In 1968, we put together one organization for women of color called Black Women Organized for Political Action. One of the things we did in that organization was find a new way to come up with leadership. The leadership issue was important because women were not in a lot of places, so they really did not know how to deal with politics. Very few women were in Congress in those days. Very few women were at the state level in politics, too, so we had to get them to think, "I can go into politics."

Because what we found was there would be one person up there doing everything, and everybody else was sitting back while that one person was doing everything. Everyone else was being nice, but not necessarily doing anything beyond being nice. So I figured, and so did other people who were working with me, that we needed to broaden the group. We couldn't just have the same people doing it all the time. There was so much to do that they would be falling down and not able to get it all done. So we said, "We've got to build more leadership. There's no question of it."

The solution we came up with was to change the way we organized that group so that we would have a change in leadership every quarter. Every three months, you would stop having the same person who was the president or the vice president or the treasurer, and new people had to come in. Those new people would have three months again to do what they would do. People said, "That's crazy, they won't know how to do this. Suppose they do something stupid?" And I said, "How much stupid can you do in three months?

They will learn one thing, though: that if you're going to do this, you should be in leadership. Because no one person can do this." So people came in and took on this approach.

We built a whole lot of new leaders who came in. A lot of young women, and a lot of older women who hadn't been asked to do anything except in the church, and that was the only place that they were gonna do anything. We got them to come in, and they learned how to be politicians, they learned how elections were put together, they learned how to run a meeting. They learned how to take a chance on doing something that they had never done before and watch it work.

We really saw women change magically. They would come in, and they wouldn't know how to do this, and they wouldn't know how to do that. But if you show them that leadership really means that you've got to do something, they're gonna change. Some people who had come in were so quiet, you would hardly see them. By the time the three months was over, they had learned a lot. That you've got to work at it. You can't sit back and watch the person who is "the leader" doing it all, because we have to constantly have leadership. We grew a lot of women who were fabulous. They were just marvelous. You wanted to cry after you'd seen in three months how much change there would be.

It was just amazing to see. Because you would see these women blooming. The woman who would not talk at all suddenly had an idea, and she knew what she wanted to do and she did it. Or she took a chance on what she wanted to have done, and then she found out that it worked. So all of a sudden she's now a leader, because she did this and it's working and we're doing okay. For the first time, I think women began to see that it was useful to get involved in politics. We just didn't say, "All the white women are going to be over here, and all the black people are going to be here, and the Latinas are going to be here." We said, "We've got to come together. We've got to figure out what is it that we all have in common with each other. What

do we have in common that brings us together?" We got more wom-
en involved in politics as a result of trying to do something on the
issues of women from the point of view of the feminist approaches.
You have to do something about politics. These things are done by
changing laws, and you have to get the people in the book who are
going to go with you when the law comes up for change.

My organizing background was really helpful, because I had
learned along that whole route that you had to keep bringing new
people in. You couldn't assume that they were just gonna find you
somewhere, and show up and have the major changes in the society. You had to work at certain things. We even set up a credit union
for women. For all women, not just black women or white women.
We put together a committee that was divided in all kinds of race
and ethnicity and power and all the rest, and they came together
and they worked together.

I was not the only one who worked on framing the issue and
gathering support. We kept finding people who would work on that.
It was important not to assume that everybody would understand
why we were doing this and how we were doing it. We had to do
a little education. For a lot of women who had never been invited
into politics at the high levels, we had to tell them, "You should
be in there, because that's where the decisions are made." And it
worked. It was amazing to me that it worked. But it was because we
had all of these things happening at the same time. I've seen it in
the Latino community, I've seen it in the Asian community, where
the women, again, who had never had an opportunity to do any of
these things—never thought they could do it—get out there in the
middle of something and do an incredible job. Because somehow or
other, they had been listening and knew that there was something
that they could do, and they were gonna do it.

We did studies in various states which showed that women were
not getting the same amount of money as men for the jobs that they
did. We looked at all of the data that we had out there: How many

women were there in Congress? Forget Congress, how many are in your state? How many are in your city? This is where we decided to go. At one point, right here in San Francisco, we got to the point where we had six women out of eleven spots on our board of supervisors because we reached out and we began to come together. We have never had six women since on the San Francisco Board of Supervisors. But we did it at that point in time because it was new and people were ready to move on it.

We also learned how to work with each other. We put on a conference in the Bay Area in 1982 called Black Women: Toward a Strategy for the Twenty-First Century. We pulled these groups of women from all over the place that we had gotten leadership from, and we decided on a conference to look at issues that we needed to talk about. Over five hundred women came to that conference over in Berkeley. The first day was spent discussing the history of women who are leaders. We had a play that was put together by some of our members about black women in history. The next day, we formed thirty-two separate meeting groups on all kinds of issues. Attendees picked out the issues they wanted, came and talked with each other, and came up with policies that have gotten out into a whole lot of other places now. They don't need me anymore. There are lots of people around who are doing things.

We called conferences, too. We had about four or five African American committees that we put together here in California. It was very important to do that. Most of the women were not getting involved, and the people of color who were getting involved were mostly men. The women were not out there. So we began to put groups together. We started calling them all kinds of things. One discussion group we set up in the Bay Area in 1984 was something called Black Women Stirring the Waters.

We used this beautiful picture of Sojourner Truth on the first publicity material that we put out for the group, with the quotes that she made when she was dealing with women's issues as one of a very small group of black women who were working on women's suffrage in her era. We selected Sojourner Truth because she had been early on the issue of equal opportunity, and had said things that we could easily get out and have women say, "Sure, I can do that. I can be part of it. I'm a citizen of the United States and I ought to be able to do this." We connected the suffragist movement with what we were now doing on the economic level, and brought the two things together.

Things were happening that made it a lot more possible to make changes. When you find yourself in a room with 250 women for a meeting, and you are seeing all the things happening in your country, you figure: let me get a few more things into this meeting as long as I've got all these people here. Let's try to talk about what we still have to do. What are the things that still are out there to be done, and who's going to do it? Nobody's going to sit and do it all for you if you're not ready to get up there and do some of it for yourself. Then it happens.

It was timing. We met with success because we had the time to do it, in a lot of ways. Or we had always had the time and never used it well enough because nobody was saying there's something to be done that's really important. We could have tried some of these things at a different time in history and we would not have been able to get very far on them. But we were lucky that we had some things that had happened that gave us something to stand on, and then we just kept standing up a little higher until we weren't just sitting down and doing nothing; we were standing up and doing a whole lot of other things.

Women were not always behind the scenes in the Civil Rights Movement. They were doing some significant work at that time. There are heroines, when you start looking at the history, and we learned a lot from a whole lot of people that were one hundred years before us.

They say Rosa Parks was a person working in here, and she was in the bus and they wanted her to move, and that's it. That's what you know about her, and that's the end of it. You don't hear about all the other things that she did all along, or how she decided what she was gonna do. She was in a very dangerous place when she did this. No, it's, "She just happened to be on the bus and that was it."

Pauli Murray was great, and Maida Springer was great. Maida was really one of the people that I admired when I was with the union. We crossed paths frequently. We would be at conferences together, so we talked a lot. I knew Maida very well, and she was one of my heroines because she had been there way before I had gotten into the union movements. She was out there and she was doing really great stuff in a very real way, across all of the racial groups, too. Maida was amazing because she not only worked in the union movement here; she did it internationally before it was something that people thought that you could do.

I think African American women who have made marks on society tend to think of "us" rather than "me." That was true in the Civil Rights Movement as well. You almost never heard much about the women in the Civil Rights Movement, because it was always the men that were out there in the big places. Most of the women weren't thinking about themselves. They were thinking about "us," not "me."

I believe in "we." We ought to put these people out there in so many ways so that everybody feels, "I can do it." Because one of the reasons I think a lot of people don't get in is they have gotten to the point where they believe, because nobody has told them otherwise, that they can't do it. That they don't have the skills to do it. But there were these women, and there were these men, and there were these young kids who went and did it because they felt that they had to be part of this.

You have to find others that are doing things that help you under-stand what you might be able to do. Because we have not really given women in particular a lot of opportunity to think about what they want to do. There's an idea that you're not successful unless you have a husband who has done this or that. So that's the whole glory. You have to wear certain kinds of clothes. You have to do all of these things. But then you find somebody who isn't doing all of that, but who is doing incredible stuff to make change in this society. We need to get women doing things beyond what we're giving them now, because they have the ability to do it.

I think women are educators in a lot of ways because that's what they have been trained to do. Whether it's an actual program or not, they're expected to play a major part with the children in their families, and make sure they get educated along the way. Fathers usually had to go to work and didn't always have time to spend on these issues, even though they loved their children just like everybody else. But they had other things to do. My mother never worked outside the home until the war, when she went into the industry because she was a good seamstress. Behind the scenes, women were doing everything. They were raising the money, they were getting out there and getting into all the communities and making sure the people knew where things were going. They were training as they went along. I was working at the California Fair Employment Practice Commission in the early 1960s, and I did training of the youngsters that went into the marches that were going on in the South. I couldn't go to the South because I was working here and I couldn't get away. I needed to stay here and work and earn my money. But what we did was what we could do.

We trained a lot of the people from the West who went all the way to the East to march in all those marches. We told them, "Do not think for a minute that these people in the East don't know what this is all about. Don't go and say, 'I'm from California and I know more than you do,' because you don't. You don't know what it's like to be there. So when you go there, you're gonna dress in the best kind of way you can, you're gonna be polite to everybody, and you are changing the world by doing this." A lot of people did go on that basis. A number of them really never came back because some of them died in some of those places.

The Civil Rights Movement, to me, was the beginning of really making the United States what it's always thought it was, which was a country which was really concerned about all people in the society. I'm not sure that I care whether I'm remembered, but I would like to think for myself that what I did during my life is useful, in terms of what I had been brought up to believe our country needed to do to change. Part of it was that I wanted to be part of the changes. I wanted to be sure that I was out there doing whatever I could do, and to try new ways of getting things done.

I think we've spent so much time training our young people to go to great schools, make a lot of money, and take over the country. The attitude is, "You can't trust these people who aren't in great schools, who don't have a lot of money. They don't know what they're doing, so we have to do it for them." People have been living for a long time, and a lot of people can do a lot of things. In fact, I have found people of poverty who have got themselves organized can do better at some of these issues that we're talking about than some of the people who have been separated by the way in which we plan our cities, and where we put our factories. You get a very different thing from those kinds of persons.

There are a lot of people who brought a lot of stuff to me that I didn't know about because I hadn't been in those communities at those times. So I think until we reach out and touch everybody that you could possibly touch, we don't know what's going on. We have to rely on somebody else telling us what's happening. And then we find out later, they didn't do that at all. They did something else. So, democracy is hard, because it requires you to know what's going on and to be part of whatever the changes are gonna be.

Nobody is gonna come in and make something marvelous for you unless it's also making it marvelous for them. Both groups should know that. So the very rich and the very poor should really come together, because they need both of them to sit down and figure out what needs to be done and for whom as we go along. Because if we have something that is going to benefit one group and then put the other group even further down on the bottom, they're not going to want it, because it doesn't give them anything in return. Democracy is supposed to have everybody use their talents and do all the things to make it work.

I love to see the changes. I love to see the young people coming in and being able to pick up and keep moving forward. Learning that it's not about you and it's not about me, but it is about much bigger issues. If we're going to be a democracy in this country, it's going to require that we find ways of opening all people to understanding that they not only have power, but they have responsibility. I think there's been a big change in San Francisco because of that. Not because of me, again, but because of people deciding that you do have to work. If you get out there, you can't just go around and say, "Where's the food?" When you come, you're gonna have to do some work.

It's been marvelous to get in and meet these people and see how much has happened in places that you thought nothing was going to happen for a long time. And then to see, which is happening now, crossing the lines. You're not just seeing people who are talking about "my group." The recognition is that it has got to be big. All of us who have the philosophy need to come together, and we need to find people that we can make changes with and have ideas about what the changes ought to be. I believe that has to happen internationally as well. But first, I think we've got to get the United States in the right position.

Aileen Clarke Hernandez attends the PBS Winter TCA Tour at the Langham Huntington Hotel on January 15, 2013, in Pasadena, California. (Credit: AP Photo / Richard Shotwell)

Diane Nash in Chicago, July 20, 1960. (Credit: AP Photo)

4

DIANE NASH

Born in 1938 in Chicago, Diane Nash became one of the recognized student leaders of the Civil Rights Movement after leaving Howard University in Washington, D.C., and transferring to Fisk University in Nashville, Tennessee. Raised in a middle-class Catholic home in Chicago, Nash's early years in Chicago included applying to charm school, like many girls and young women at that time. Although beautiful and well-spoken, Nash was rejected because of her race. That negative experience proved relatively mild when she encountered segregation as a Howard student and then witnessed and protested the brutal segregation in Nashville.

She was elected chairperson of the Nashville Sit-In Movement, formed to desegregate Nashville lunch counters before the founding of the Student Nonviolent Coordinating Committee (SNCC). The Nashville Sit-In Movement continued the Freedom Ride after the Congress of Racial Equality (CORE) was forced to discontinue it. Her tactical and unwavering support of the Freedom Riders was critical to their success. She coordinated the Birmingham, Alabama, to Jackson, Mississippi, Freedom Ride. Nash's reputation as reliable and relentlessly diligent led to her election as head of the Nashville student movement in 1960 and 1961. She chose to adhere to the protest policy of "jail without bail" when arrested for supporting the Rock Hill, South Carolina, students' lunch counter protest. Her resolve gained support from the community as well as the press coverage needed to shine a light on the reason for the student protests.

She was pregnant when she went to jail in Mississippi in the spring of 1962. In April 1962, Martin Luther King Jr. nominated her for an award from the NAACP's New York branch, acknowledging her as the "driving spirit in the nonviolent assault on segregation at lunch counters" (Martin Luther King Jr. Research and Education Institute, n.d., para. 1).

In the PBS documentary *Freedom Riders*, Nash told of her firm stance against succumbing to the violence that greeted civil rights protesters:

> It was clear to me that if we allowed the Freedom Ride to stop . . . after so much violence had been inflicted, the message would have been sent that all you have to do to stop a nonviolent campaign is inflict massive violence. (American Experience Films & Nelson, 2010)

After Nash's work with the Freedom Riders, she returned to her home of Chicago and became a tenant organizer. I interviewed Nash by telephone.

The Nashville Student Movement

I grew up on the Southside of Chicago, which was segregated. But there were no signs that were "white" and "colored." When I went to college at Fisk University in Nashville, I did encounter more overt segregation, such as signs in restaurants and libraries, and public accommodations that blacks could not use or had to use back doors. That kind of thing. Of course, the whole purpose of segregation was to convince you that you were "less than" and not worthy of using facilities that the general public could use, convincing black people of their own inferiority.

When I obeyed segregation rules I felt like I was agreeing to my own inferiority. That was a period of my life where I was really interested in expanding myself, going to new places, learning new things, and meeting new people. Segregation was extremely restricting, and I felt that keenly. It was humiliating. So I started looking for an organization that was trying to do something to prevent segregation. That was 1959. I was fortunate finally to find the workshop that Reverend James Lawson, a divinity student at Vanderbilt University at the time, was conducting in Nashville. In those workshops, I gained an excellent education in the philosophy and strategies of nonviolence. I consider myself very fortunate and blessed that I had the opportunity. It was life-changing for me.

We established a central committee—the Student Central Committee is what we called it—in Nashville, and that was the committee that gave guidance to the sit-ins at restaurants and lunch counters. That was in 1960. The Student Central Committee was made of representatives from each of the colleges and universities in the Nashville metropolitan area that were participating in the Movement. There were about thirty of us, and I was elected chairperson. I was the third chairperson.

The first two were men. Each missed meetings and missed demonstrations, and when they came back, we asked them where they'd been. Both said the same thing: that they had been studying. We could not afford to have officers who were not efficient because someone could get killed or injured if we did not carry out the Movement efficiently. So we thanked them for their services and replaced them. I guess each one lasted probably a couple of weeks in office. So they elected me chairperson.

I really didn't want to be chairperson. I declined and offered every excuse I could think of, really, because I was afraid. That same evening after I was elected, I thought, "My goodness, what will have happened in the next two months? We will be coming up against, oh, man, white men in their forties and fifties and sixties who are businessmen and politicians." And here we are students. You know, seventeen, eighteen, maybe to twenty-one or twenty-two years old. It was daunting. I'm not sure I did overcome my fear. I just kept doing what had to be done. The fear was definitely there, but fear was also a great motivator, because I knew if we were not efficient someone could get killed or injured. So that fear, I think it made us extremely efficient.

That central committee of students was remarkable. There were people who were coming in just to kind of check things out. Some of them were not serious. But after the first several weeks of the Movement, when people saw that there was a core group of us who were very serious, and that you had to be serious and efficient in order to be part of us, then those who were not serious just dropped away. Of those who were left, I cannot remember a single incident where people agreed to do a task and came back when it was time to have the task completed and said, "I was not able to finish." You just did not do that, because the whole group was relying on you. If you had trouble getting your task done, you got somebody to help you. I think, again, there was certainly a fear motivation. It was fear of someone you cared a lot about getting killed or injured. Or, in addition to that, knowledge that the group wouldn't tolerate it. Keep in mind, I just said we had replaced two chairpersons because they weren't efficient. So there was an atmosphere within that group that you had to be serious or you weren't gonna be part of the group.

The thirty of us made all the decisions, and we did it with consensus. Meaning that we'd take straw votes, and if there was any real division we kept talking until everybody was in agreement, except maybe one or two, possibly three people as opposed to the other twenty-seven. When that happened, even the three people understood that that was the will of the group. We did that because we needed everybody's enthusiastic support for the things that we were doing. It was a remarkable group. All of us trained in nonviolence, and using it in our group as well as within larger Nashville.

You understand the difference between the Student Nonviolent Coordinating Committee and the Nashville Central Committee? All right. In the spring of 1960, over the Easter weekend, by that time sit-ins had begun in many, many cities throughout the South. Ms. Ella Baker, who at that time was the executive director of the Southern Christian Leadership Conference, saw that there would be value in bringing together student leaders from the many campuses and cities where sit-ins were taking place. So she organized the conference in Raleigh, North Carolina, at Shaw University, over that Easter weekend in 1960. And the students came together.

We had two needs at that conference. One, we needed a kind of a clearinghouse where information could come in from all the campuses and then be distributed or disseminated so that we could keep up with what was going on in the many cities where sit-in movements were taking place. The second thing we wanted was the ability to have coordinated demonstrations. To carry out those two paths, we elected what we named the Student Nonviolent Coordinating Committee. That was a national organization, or more specifically a southern organization of many campuses. I was elected to that coordinating committee. But that's the difference between the Nonviolent Coordinating Committee nationally and locally the

Nashville Student Central Committee. I hope that that's kind of clear.

From time to time gender discrimination was an issue I faced. The Civil Rights Movement came before the women's movement. Now, in Nashville it was not an issue at all. I won't be falsely modest at this point. I think I was elected because I had worked with the people who elected me, and we had worked together for a while. And I think I was elected because they saw that I was efficient. So I had no trouble whatsoever with gender discrimination in Nashville.

Freedom Rides and the Selma Right to Vote Movement

Two things that I think I was able to make a contribution with: one was in recognizing that the Freedom Ride had to continue.

When the people from the Congress of Racial Equality, CORE, who began the Freedom Ride, had been beaten so repeatedly and severely that they were forced to end the Freedom Ride, I was able to understand that if it had stopped at that point southern white racists would have believed that a Movement project could be stopped by inflicting a great deal of violence on it. And if that message got sent, we would've had so many people killed after that. It would've been impossible to have a movement about anything. Voting rights, desegregation, or whatever. So it was really critically important that that message not be sent, and that it be clear that you could not stop a civil rights campaign, a nonviolent campaign, by inflicting violence. So that was one thing.

The second one was in response to the four little girls being murdered in the Sixteenth Street Baptist Church in Birmingham. It was important to me that that murder not go unanswered and unaddressed. My husband at the time, James Bevel, and I that very afternoon when the little girls were killed formulated a strategy for the Southern Christian Leadership Conference to get the right to vote in Alabama. Because we felt if blacks had the right to vote in Alabama they could better protect their children. So we really pushed for that and for what became the Selma right to vote campaign.

Incidentally, we made a conscious choice that Sunday afternoon, because we felt confident that if we tried we could find out who was responsible for those murders, for that bombing, that they might get killed. And we considered that as one of the serious choices. The second choice was to have a nonviolent movement to get the right to vote, so the blacks in Alabama could better protect their children. We made a conscious choice, no matter how long it took, to work on getting the right to vote. So, the right to vote, the Selma movement, was a direct result of the little girls getting killed. And the only thing I can think of more tragic than their being murdered was if they were murdered and there was not a positive response to it. I think getting the right to vote was the best that we could do.

The Power of Nonviolence

Do not depend on elected officials to make the necessary changes in society. I think if we had waited for elected officials to desegregate lunch counters and buses and get the right to vote in the South, now fifty years later, I think we'd still be waiting. I think that if young people—and you know, any age—if citizens don't take the best interests of this country into their own hands and make the necessary changes, nonviolently, fifty years from now they still will not be made. I think one of the worst things that people have done is that they have begun to rely on elected officials to do what's necessary. And they're not gonna do it.

Nonviolence is a very powerful way to make social change without killing and maiming your fellow human being. Often, when people engage in violence their real intention is to improve things and make a better society. If that worked, with all the violence that's been used in the last several centuries even, we would be living in utopia. But violence tends to increase the problems rather than to solve them. And I think there probably was no greater invention during the twentieth century than Gandhi's invention of how to really wage warfare and change society using nonviolence.

I'm surprised that with the degree of success that we had in the sixties and the relatively few casualties—and even one casualty is far too many—but, comparing the number of casualties that we had in the nonviolent movement to the number of casualties that you have in violent attempts at social change, I really would think that people would be wise to study nonviolence, and use it. It's more efficient than just about anything I can think of.

Diane Nash, guest speaker at Memorial Chapel, University of Redlands, January 27, 2016. (Credit: Sky Ung)

Judy Richardson (center) with other SNCC staff workers during a sit-in at the Toddle House restaurant in Atlanta, shortly before their arrest. December 1963. (Credit: Danny Lyon)

5

JUDY RICHARDSON

Judy Richardson grew up in Tarrytown, New York, in an integrated working-class community. Her father was a factory worker and was the main organizer for the plant's United Auto Workers local. When Richardson was seven, her father had a heart attack and died "on the line." As a result, she was raised by her mother, who became a full-time office clerk and who introduced her to issues of social justice.

During her freshman year at Swarthmore College, Richardson joined the Students for a Democratic Society (SDS) group on campus that was organizing against segregation in nearby Chester, Pennsylvania, and in Cambridge, Maryland. She left Swarthmore (and forfeited her four-year scholarship) after her freshman year to join the staff of the Student Nonviolent Coordinating Committee (SNCC). She worked in SNCC's national office in Atlanta and on SNCC's voter registration and social justice projects in Georgia, Mississippi, and Alabama. She also helped monitor SNCC's twenty-four-hour, 800-like telephone line—literally a lifeline for SNCC activists throughout the rural South. Her experiences in SNCC continue to profoundly shape her life, both professionally and personally.

Richardson later co-founded Drum and Spear Bookstore and Drum and Spear Press in Washington, D.C. Both institutions were instrumental in publishing and promoting black literature. As children's book editor for the press, she facilitated publication of the first book by noted children's book author Eloise Greenfield, whose manuscript had been previously rejected by numerous publishers.

Since then, Greenfield has published more than forty books for young readers.

Richardson has spent a lifetime using communications and education as tools for social justice. In the 1970s—as part of the many community projects begun by Drum and Spear—she helped originate and host a popular children's radio program as the character Bibi Amina to introduce children to black children's literature and African folktales. She later became the series associate producer and education director for *Eyes on the Prize*, the seminal fourteen-hour PBS series on the Civil Rights Movement. She, in fact, is partially responsible for the compelling name. She continued to work on racial justice issues with the United Church of Christ Commission for Racial Justice and through her film and education work. She has produced numerous films for broadcast and museums, focused on African American history. She was also co-editor of *Hands on the Freedom Plow*, an anthology of the writings of fifty-two courageous SNCC women. She was awarded an honorary doctorate by Swarthmore College and was a distinguished visiting professor at Brown University. She is also on the board of the SNCC Legacy Project, which collaborates with Duke University and others on SNCC's legacy and continuing work on contemporary issues, including a website (www.SNCCdigital.org), and work with the Movement for Black Lives and progressive educational organizations. She continues to lecture, write, and conduct teacher workshops about the Movement then and now. This interview took place at her home in Cambridge, Massachusetts.

Directed Toward the Movement

My participation in the Movement changed my life. I grew up in Tarrytown, New York, in the "under the hill" section of Tarrytown, where working-class black and white people lived. My father had helped organize the United Auto Workers local at the Fisher Body plant, where they made parts for Chevrolet cars. Everyone just called it "the plant." You could tell time from the shifts at the plant. My father was treasurer of that local. When I was seven, he died on the assembly line.

After my father's death, my mother became a working single parent. Now, she had an eighth-grade education, but she read everything. She read the *New York Post* when it was still a real newspaper. She watched *Meet the Press*.

I was only peripherally aware of racial discrimination growing up in Tarrytown. In Tarrytown, it was mainly housing discrimination. It was also where they put black students in school. In seventh grade, for example, they put me in secretarial classes. It was assumed that black students would go into secretarial work. There was only one other black student on the academic track, and she was a senior when I was a freshman.

My mother raised holy hell. At that point, my sister was at Bennington College on a full scholarship, and I was toward the top of my class. But in my secretarial classes is where I learned to type ninety words a minute, and write Gregg shorthand. So it did serve me in good stead later on. I could take college notes very quickly, and other kinds of notes. These skills also helped in SNCC. When I arrived at Swarthmore College (outside of Philadelphia) as a freshman, I got involved with the Swarthmore Political Action Committee, SPAC, a chapter of Students for a Democratic Society (SDS). They were working with the all-black cafeteria staff in Swarthmore's dining room, not so much to unionize them, but to help organize them. The staff had already started protesting for a livable wage.

I was on a full four-year scholarship and so was work-study and working as a student in the dining room. People are used to bussing their own stuff now, but this was a time when Swarthmore students were served in this wonderful dining hall on Swarthmore's campus. As part of the cafeteria staff, I would come in and I would bring the meals to those who were seated and then take the empty trays back. I did that two or three days a week as part of my work-study responsibilities. I was part of that cafeteria staff, but I was not the same because I'm a student. I'm not working there nor am I vulnerable in the same way.

One of the things the nonstudent cafeteria workers had tried to do was get this humongous water boiler that was uncovered in the dining room covered. A lot of the women—the waitresses were all black women—would bump up against it as they were trying to rush getting all these meals to the students. They kept trying to get this pipe covered, and Swarthmore never did anything about it. However, when *I* bumped into it, the dean called me in: "Is there anything you need?" And the thing is, that pipe was so hot that for years afterward, truly, I had "H2O" on the back of my calf because it had been seared into it. Backwards though. The SPAC folks said, "So, this is what we want. They are obviously going to pay more attention to you because you are a student, you're not just a worker." Immediately, they covered that pipe.

Then we brought forward the whole thing about a living wage. There was this amazing waitress. She was fiery. She was the kind of person, when you're organizing, who you really want on the team. She would come to all the SPAC meetings and she would talk about what the women were doing. Other women from the cafeteria staff were also coming to the SPAC meetings because of what SPAC was doing to work with them on getting a living wage. That was one issue they organized around.

The other thing SPAC was working on—in Chester, Pennsylvania—was protesting the horrible schools that were in the black community at the time. Still are. As a matter of fact, at Obama's State of the Union in 2012, he acknowledged a black teacher from Chester, Pennsylvania. The state had cut off the funds to the schools. The teachers in Chester said they would continue teaching even though they had not gotten the contract they were fighting for. They said, "We will continue teaching because we want to continue working with the young people that are in Chester." That's the same Chester that had bad schools then, that has bad schools now.

There were two co-chairs of SPAC at the time. One was Mimi Feingold. The other was Carl Wittman. Mimi had come back from the 1961 Freedom Rides and had served six weeks in the Mississippi State Penitentiary, the dreaded Parchman Farm, where people went in and never came back out again. She goes into Louisiana with CORE and if there was any place worse than Mississippi it was swampy Louisiana. I mean, it was horrible. She also did a lot of work in the Movement after she left Swarthmore. When Carl Wittman left Swarthmore, they got married. But he's gay, so that didn't work out. They split, and he then goes to San Francisco and writes this major treatise for gay rights. He later died of AIDS. I read a moving account of how people came by his window to pay homage to Carl while he was dying.

I didn't know anything about Mimi's work in Mississippi or Louisiana at the time. I had no idea, because I'm new. I'm just coming from Tarrytown. I don't know from nothing. I just get pulled into this because I'm trying to see what I can get into. My mother's not there to stop me. So what happens is that I find out about the campaign that the Swarthmore group is working on. I find out that they're doing a bus ride with Swarthmore students down to Cambridge, Maryland, on the Eastern Shore of Maryland, and I get on the bus.

In Cambridge, I find a very different kind of discrimination, one that I was just peripherally aware of in Tarrytown. SPAC is working with this amazing local leader, Gloria Richardson, no kin to me, who was the most prominent leader of a very strong community group called CNAC, the Cambridge Nonviolent Action Committee. Gloria and the organizing committee were inviting local college students to come in and help them not only to desegregate the public facilities there, but also to protest discriminatory hiring, because the hiring was so segregated. Black people did not have access to a lot of the jobs.

SNCC

In the fall of 1963, I took what was supposed to be only a six-month leave of absence from Swarthmore to join SNCC's Atlanta office. I was on the WATS line—the Wide Area Telephone Service—like an 800 line. When somebody called in . . . there are people who remember me from when they would call in, because we had this thing where you had to call in every couple of hours so we knew that you all were still alive and what was going on.

Keeping calm was one of those things that I learned in the Movement. How you keep calm when people are saying things like, "They just shot into the Freedom House." I would get all the information, then call the FBI, depending on where the incident was. Before '64 there is no FBI office in Mississippi. The sequence was to call the FBI, then to call John Doar at the Justice Department, then to call one of SNCC's northern support folks or whomever, but to stay calm and get all of the detailed information. To ask about how many people, get all that down, and disseminate that information to those who might or might not do anything with it.

Even the secretarial skills were helpful. I remember sitting there transcribing Prathia Hall, who was the first female field secretary. She'd come out of an evangelical church that her mother and father had in Philly. Prathia was an amazing preacher. Dr. King even said,

"I don't want to follow Prathia." Prathia goes into Selma, Alabama. She was also assistant project director with Charles Sherrod in Albany in southwest Georgia. I remember sitting in that teeny tiny little office on 8½ Raymond Street in Atlanta and transcribing her speech on those big green mimeograph stencils. Tears just rolling down my cheeks because she was so powerful.

Well, I couldn't speak like that. What I *could* do was transcribe it. I had the skills to do that. The kind of things I've done since then are more related to how do you get the message out about who we were, what we did, and why we did it as young people in SNCC. But that's after, because back then I couldn't speak in front of a mass meeting. I just couldn't do it. I was afraid of public speaking.

At one point I and some of the other women staffers staged a half-serious protest in Jim Forman's [SNCC's executive secretary] office over the fact that no men ever took meeting minutes. I just know for me, I was tired of taking all the minutes and notes for those long staff meetings that would last three days. SNCC people . . . we were young, and we could talk forever. The photo that was taken of the protest was really a re-creation. What happened is, after the actual sit-in, Danny Lyon, a SNCC photographer, says to get back together so he can document it by taking a photo. So we come back together and Forman has this little sign and we have our picket signs and stuff. I don't remember who organized the actual sit-in.

The skills that I had acquired up to that point got nurtured in SNCC. My writing skills got nurtured. When Julian Bond is convinced to run for the new open seat in Atlanta for the Georgia House of Representatives, Charlie Cobb and Ivanhoe Donaldson become the campaign managers. They want to test what does it mean for SNCC people to run for regular office, aside from the Mississippi Freedom Democratic Party, which was against the all-white Mississippi Democratic Party delegation to the Democratic Convention in 1968. Can they bring the values and organizing techniques we had in SNCC into organizing for political office. So now we're going for the seat with Julian in this new district in Atlanta, and I came out of SNCC's Lowndes County, Alabama, project to run the office. That's what I could do, because I can administer; I can organize that way. I had certain skills, but I wasn't going to be speaking.

When Julian gets the seat, I become the temporary director of communications. But it was like rolling off a log then, because Julian and the communications department had a system. There was very little I had to do to get the SNCC newsletter out.

Ella Baker's Influence

Ella Baker was amazing. I'll say to teachers, "You may never know the impact you're making on some of your students." Because for me, Ms. Baker was that influential teacher. I watched how Ms. Baker moved, and first of all, she always wanted to know, "Who are your people?" I saw her do that in meetings. Part of that was she wanted to know what connections you had. What is your community? How were you raised? So when she does this to someone like Ruth Howard Chambers, she finds out that Ruth Howard's people were from Rocky Mount, North Carolina. Ruth may have grown up in Washington, D.C., but she spent her summers with relatives in Rocky Mount, North Carolina. And that's where Miss Baker grew up, in that same area. So she said, "Oh, who's your—" and they connect that way. So, it was always, "Who are your people" when she meets you.

The kind of history that she transfers and translates to us—the contacts she gives us as we're doing our work—was key. The reason Bob Moses goes to Amzie Moore in McComb, Mississippi, is because Ms. Baker says, "You need to go to Amzie if this is what you're looking for." Then Amzie says, "I'm not ready for you here, you need to go to southwest Mississippi. C. C. Bryant is ready for you." It's this passing on of the knowledge but also the contacts that come, particularly with the black World War II vets.

Ms. Baker was kind of a behind-the-scenes leader, unless she saw things going wrong, in which case she would come to the floor. In one meeting that I took minutes for, she's asking the director of SNCC's northern support office in the Atlanta office about saying Dick Gregory had said that he would do fundraising for us, but he needed to be paid. Now, Harry Belafonte gave us five parties. He said he would ask for no money and go to five parties on Long Island. My sister, Carita, as a matter of fact, coordinated those parties out of SNCC's New York office. But Belafonte didn't charge. Dick Gregory though, at the beginning of '64, is saying he'll give us that, but he wants $10,000. It could have been for his transportation and all that, but the problem that Ms. Baker then raises is, "Well, if we do this, what kind of precedent does it set? Because other people are doing pro bono work. There are a lot of folks who are just giving this to us. So what does that mean?"*

She also steps in and speaks to the SNCC people who are working with high school kids through the Atlanta Project. She asked, "Do the parents always know when their kids are going to jail? You have got to make sure that you contact the parents so they have a relationship with you."

So she's stepping in at these places. She's talking to SNCC people who are organizing the Atlanta University Center, Spelman, Clark, Morehouse, and Atlanta University, and at one point she says, and it's one of my favorite lines, "You cannot go on the campus in these denims. You have to deal with the pseudo-sophistication of the Negro college student." It was funny—"the pseudo-sophistication." I love it. It's not that Ms. Baker is putting people down, because she has an abiding respect for black folks, but she is saying, "They

---

* Dick Gregory was a major contributor to civil rights causes and organizations.

think they know it all coming out of Spelman and Morehouse." But she's saying also, "You cannot organize them in the dress that you're using to organize with sharecroppers in Leflore County, Mississippi. You've got to dress differently."

In the same way, she kept the group together when SNCC was about to split in 1961, with the direct action people separating from the voter registration people. She explains, "You can do both of these things." It's after a few days of meetings, and SNCC is about to break apart, but she helps to get this compromise together.

Ms. Baker was the age at the time that I am now as I think back on her. I look at what she went through with us, and it's amazing. She had bronchial problems. She had asthma, and everybody was smoking. I wasn't smoking because I couldn't take it, but everybody was smoking. So she would have this little mask over her nose and mouth. She would be up with us until three or four in the morning. It's amazing to me.

I watched her move, and I watched when she inserted herself and when she didn't. I remember we had an Executive Committee meeting in Atlanta at Frazier's Restaurant, which was down from Paschal's Restaurant. Paschal's was about money. The Paschal brothers, you really needed to have the money if you wanted to have breakfast there. We only made ten dollars a week, which was $9.64 after taxes. And there were weeks when we didn't get any money. But you could go to Mr. Frazier, though [owner of Frazier's Restaurant, down the street from Paschal's], and he would feed you. So we had meetings in Mr. Frazier's basement. He was just down on Hunter Street—now King Drive. This Exec Committee meeting got really contentious, and something happened in a very personal way—a domestic thing. It broke up the meeting temporarily, and Ms. Baker went to the staff person to whom this had happened and wanted to know what's going on, not to get into the person's business, but more to find out, "How is this affecting your work?"

She somehow knew how to say the right thing. It was always with questions, though. It was kind of like, "If you do this now, what's going to happen ten months from now?" As young people who normally wouldn't think past three weeks, she tried to get us to think forward a year from now. There were a lot of things at stake in terms of what we were doing. If you're trying to get black people registered to vote without getting them killed, then how do you organize in a way that thinks ahead? Is the community ready for what you are doing? Is this what the community wants? Because before you ever did anything, you're sitting on their porch and talking to them about stuff, particularly around the right to vote and how is this going to change things for you. It was grassroots organizing. She grew up with it. It was a part of her.

Strength

My strength comes from the people around me. In the Movement, it also came from the songs. Although I don't come from a religious background, when someone like Mrs. Fannie Lou Hamer starts singing "I'm a Soldier in the Army," or any of that, it takes you to another place and can't nobody touch you. You can be on a demonstration. You're singing. They can't touch you. As Dr. Bernice Johnson Reagon has said, it's almost like you put up a wall with your song.

When you got tired, there were always people who just said, "Okay, we've got to keep going. We've got to get this newsletter out. We've got to get this done." Sometimes people would say things that would make you feel like you could do anything. It wasn't just the music. You would hear somebody say something in a mass meeting that was just amazing.

And I'll say, sometimes strength was just because you're mad. When they started shooting at us in Greenwood, Mississippi, in the summer of 1964, I thought it was a backfire. But June Johnson said, "No, they're shooting at us. Hurry up." When I drive up to this hospital in Greenwood, there was a small white mob. Then, after we entered, the mob threw a brick through the picture window. There are six FBI men at the hospital because two young activists, Silas and Jake McGhee, had gotten injured. The FBI men go behind the wall, out of the way of the waiting room area, and I go, too, and then I start screaming at them to "do something!" Then I go back, and I peek around and see that the mob has gone back into the parking lot. I return to the waiting area and start putting my dimes into the telephone because I'm trying to call John Doar [at the Justice Department]. I keep trying to call. That's not because I have any great courage. It's because I'm mad as hell. First of all, I just screamed at these FBI agents because they're not doing diddly-squat. Which is usually what they didn't do—diddly-squat. Then I can't get to John Doar. And . . . I'm mad at these white racists.

One of the other things we always understood in SNCC: it isn't about individual white racists; it's about white supremacy. It's about the good members of the Chamber of Commerce, and the mayors, and all these good white people who are going to these all-white churches. It's the same thing today. The lessons that I learned then, I've taken to now. Police brutality isn't just because someone didn't have enough sensitivity training. It's because of a racist New York Police Department. We got that in SNCC.

So for me, yeah, I'm mad at these FBI agents, but I'm also mad that you've got this white mob outside. This black paratrooper, the McGhee brothers' brother, has come home from the war, from serving his country. He's in the hospital because it's his brother who has just had a rock thrown through a car window at him and has glass in his eye because he tried to go to a supposedly desegregated movie theater in downtown Greenwood. Part of what fuels me is anger. It's also all the strength I get from the wonderful people who just made me feel good and always made me feel I was valued.

Residential Freedom School

In the summer of 1965, I and others in SNCC organized a Residential Freedom School. I came up with the idea based on Charlie Cobb's idea for Freedom Schools during the 1964 Freedom Summer. I decided I want to do something similar. This was after we'd gone through Mississippi. I'd been in Mississippi the summer of 1964, Lowndes County and Selma, Alabama, in 1965, and then southwest Georgia also in '65. At some point, all of this gets kind of conflated.

My idea was that the young people from the southern movement who were still hopeful and still understood that they could make change could get together with northern kids who understood that the North was just "up South" and who needed to be infected with this sense that you *can* change this stuff. So if you got these two groups of people together, the reality of what racism really was and how national it was would come to the southern kids, and the southern kids would give the northern kids the sense that you can do something about this.

We had kids from Cambridge, Maryland, and a couple of other places in the South. We did a three-week session in Chicago with some of the guys from the projects in Chicago, and then we moved down and did just a week in Cordele, Georgia, in southwest Georgia.

During the Residential Freedom School, I remember there was a young guy named Profit who had come up from one of the southern projects. We had shown the film *Viva Zapata!*, which was great, though it's a shame they couldn't have gotten someone other than Marlon Brando—like a Chicano—to play Zapata. In SNCC, we always understood the commonality of the struggle with Nicaragua and stuff that was going on in Mexico then. Profit talked about what he saw—particularly how Zapata stayed with the people and wasn't going to take the buyout that somebody had suggested. So for Profit, who was this young guy, it was like when the lightbulb goes off and you realize, "Oh they got it!"

For me, coming out of Tarrytown, New York, what surprised me was not just the courage and traditional wisdom, but the intelligence of regular black folk in the South. Could be unschooled, but had an intelligence I would not have understood if I had just stayed in Tarrytown. I had to acknowledge it. I said, "These people are some smart people." It was amazing. Strategically and making us think differently about things, that was surprising.

Drum and Spear

Charlie Cobb and Courtland Cox and others with whom I had worked in SNCC started the Drum and Spear Bookstore in 1968, particularly Charlie, in Washington, D.C. Then they invite me to come in and administrate, and I do that.

Drum and Spear becomes the largest black bookstore in the country. I founded the children's department at Drum and Spear. There were black studies departments at Cornell and San Francisco State and wherever, so we were selling to them, too. But there had been no children's section, and I got really into children's books. Drum and Spear became a place where folks know they can get children's books. Vivian Johnson, who was working on a wonderful program in Boston in Roxbury with black kids, she's coming down to D.C. and looking at our children's section. She had an educational consulting firm called Circle Associates. We also started doing a children's radio program at WOL, which was the major black radio station in D.C., working with Dewey Hughes, who was a co-owner of the station. We did a half-hour show, on Saturdays, called *Sa Yaa Watoto*. I was Bibi Amina, and Bibi Amina would tell children's stories. I would come on and I would say, "Good morning, my young brothers and sisters. This is Bibi Amina speaking to you from

Sa Yaa Watoto, which means 'The Children's Hour' in the African language of Swahili." Then I would go on. We had people from Topper Carew's organization, The New Thing Art and Architecture Center, who did the African drumming. Mimi Hayes, who was one of the only black people I knew who had gone through Annenberg, knew radio broadcast. Together, we would do these scripts for these half-hour radio programs. We did African stories that had real meaning, as most African folktales do. We sometimes also adapted black children's books.

Then I switch over to Drum and Spear Press and I become the children's editor. At that point, there weren't many black presses. I think we had Drum and Spear Press and Broadside Press out of Detroit. But Broadside only did poetry, so we really were the only one doing other kinds of publishing. We got sent a lot of manuscripts. Because I was children's editor, I was getting lots of children's books.

I remember I was up on the top of the third floor, right in the Adams Morgan section of D.C. Right at the corner of 18th and Belmont. We had a triple-decker. Jimmy the Rat had the kitchen. I had put up a notice that said, "Jimmy the Rat has this. Go in at your own peril." There was a point when we didn't have money for heating oil, so it was really cold because it was winter. We worked up on the third floor, and Mimi was usually at the desk across from me. I remember this one night, sitting there alone, it's eight o'clock at night, I'm cold as hell, and I can't go in the kitchen because Jimmy the Rat has the kitchen. Remember D.C. rats were huge. I mean humongous. Anyway, I'm sitting up there and I get this manuscript from Eloise Greenfield. Eloise Greenfield *now* has forty, fifty children's books, all focused on black children. She's got umpteen awards and an honorary doctorate. She's on major trade publishing companies' lists. But at that point she had never published before.

The manuscript is about a little black child, a boy, who learns to read his first three words. He's so excited, and he can't wait to tell his mother. Those words are, "I can read." He puts them on a little piece of paper and he sticks it in the bottom in the back of his shoe. In my mind, he's striding off. I read it and think, "This is so cute! I love this!" Because I've already been reading these other children's books at Drum and Spear Bookstore and buying them for the store.

I call Eloise that night, and I say, "Oh, Ms. Greenfield, this is Judy Richardson, I'm at Drum and Spear. I'm sorry to call you so late, but we want to publish your book." She was so excited, because she had been rejected by about thirty-some publishers who didn't understand how wonderful this book was. It wasn't illustrated, that was the thing. It was just the text. So we got Eric Marlow, the art director at Topper's New Thing Art and Architecture Center, to do the illustrations.

Charlie Cobb's aunt hosted the launch party. Charlie comes out of a family deeply connected to black education. It's not just that his father was the head and founder of the United Church of Christ Commission for Racial Justice. His mother was chair of the Department of Romance Languages at Howard University, spoke five languages and stuff. His aunt, Charlotte Brooks, was superintendent of English for the D.C. public schools. She was the first to expose me to the idea that Black English was just like another language. The way she taught it—and asked her teachers to teach it—was, "Yes, you need to know standard English, but Black English is just as good. You need to know when to go back and forth." So, because Charlie's Aunt Charlotte is superintendent of English for the schools, we do the launch party for Eloise's book at her house up on Kansas Avenue. It was one of our first launch parties. There were a lot of people there, because all these English teachers and other teachers are coming, plus a lot of folks know Charlie's family.

The title was *Bubbles*. And on the cover—I still have it—was this little boy. You see him looking up, and there were these bubbles all over. For the launch party, I had this brilliant idea that we're going to have a bubble machine. They had wood floors. Well, I get this bubble machine working, and they all had to hold on to the walls because they were slipping all the way down these wooden floors. But it was a wonderful launch, and Eloise was so excited. She is still writing, and I keep in touch with her. She sends me all her new books, so I have a whole library of Eloise Greenfield books.

A few years ago I spoke with a young black woman who was doing something on activism in Jackson, Mississippi. She was up here at Harvard for a five-week training through the Du Bois Center. This young black woman interviewed me about my experience in Mississippi in 1964. When I meet her she says to me, "You know, I've got to tell you, you came to my class as Bibi Amina."

She grew up in D.C. She actually started tearing up on me. It was amazing. She said, "Our teachers said that we were having a special guest and you came and you had your galay"—that was when I was always in a galay* and African traditional clothes—"and you came in and you read a story as Bibi Amina." I thought, "Oh my God!" And I have no memory of it of course. She said it was the first time she had ever really seen someone in African clothing like that. I loved doing those kid's classes. They were just really cool.

Blackside Productions and Rainbow TV Works

At Blackside Productions, when I first get hired by Henry Hampton, in 1978, I knew nothing about film. Zilch. Nada. I come up to Boston because my friend Dave Lacy is coming up to be executive producer for cultural affairs at WGBH, Boston's PBS station. Henry had known of me a couple of years before that because Mimi, a mutual friend of ours, had suggested that I could be one of those that could help do a chronology of the Civil Rights Movement. So I'd given him a chronology back then, and so he hears that I'm com-

---

*Also spelled "gele." An African head wrap.

ing up to Boston, and he hired me to be the associate producer of what was going to be a one-hour documentary on the Movement, not the fourteen hours it later becomes. Henry takes a chance on me because nobody knows Blackside and he thinks that because I have Movement experience I can maybe encourage people to talk to us for interviews.

He has this title that I hated. Henry's title was "America, We Loved You Madly." Henry really was a writer. He loved the play on words of "madly." For him, there was kind of a love/hate relationship for black people with this country. So, "We loved you madly." It was what Duke Ellington used to say at the end of concerts. He would throw his arms wide and say, "I love you madly!" Henry loved it, but I hated it as a title. I kept saying that, kind of from jump. But then we get a crew on about six months later and I distribute this memo to the staff, offering alternative titles.

From the memo itself: To: Capital Cities Communications folks, Fr: Judy, Date: October 9, 1979. Re: Program Title. I just start with: "Y'all know how much I dislike the current working title. I have, therefore, perused song titles for alternatives. Here is the list. I am not wedded to any of these titles, although there are a couple I kinda like. I'm circulating this mainly to get us thinking about other possibilities. Also, since they are all related to actual freedom songs, there is a tie-in musically. Also think about reworking the below or adding your own. There is no"—underscore no—"order or preference on this listing." Okay, so I've got number one is "Moving On" then "Stayed on Freedom." Number six is "Their Eyes on the Prize" or "Keep Your Eyes on the Prize." Then I've got all the way through to twenty-two. And twenty-two has a little asterisk on it and it says, "We placed our trust in the Lord . . . (and they beat the shit out of us anyway)." And then the asterisk says, "My favorite."

Now, Henry luckily did not pick that one, but he picks "Eyes on the Prize." After *Eyes on the Prize*, I go off to Los Angeles to work with Topper Carew, because one of the things the Movement gets me on the track of is working with, if not internally black organizations, at least organizations that are working on things that I think will be of use to the black community one way or the other. Topper was African American. He was the main producer at Rainbow TV Works. They had just gotten money from the Corporation for Public Broadcasting to do a series called *The Righteous Apples*. Another project was going to be a two-hour feature film that Ivan Dixon directed. I directed the training program at Rainbow TV Works.

When I was doing research for *Eyes on the Prize*, it was different than being the producer, director, and writer for a History Channel documentary or Underground Railroad Freedom Center orientation film. But no matter what I was doing, what was best about documentary filmmaking was somehow I was lucky enough to be in an environment where they made me feel I was valued, and my skills were valued, and I was contributing to this larger mission that I had decided to join.

Skilled

I carried with me the skills I got in the Movement the rest of my life. The Movement gave me the commitment to do something connected to activism in lots of different ways and focused on the black community. I learned how to interpret the history for people.

The main thing I learned how to do is keep calm and keep things moving if that's the way it's supposed to go. One of the things that the Movement showed you was you don't let violence stop the Movement, because then they know that they can just do anything and they will stop you from doing what you're doing. No, you just keep moving. But for me it was also keeping calm. How do you assess the situation and then just keep it moving.

When I came back east, in the mid-eighties, I ended up working as director of information for the New York City–based United Church of Christ Commission for Racial Justice, which was headed by Charlie Cobb's daddy, Reverend Charles Cobb, who had started the agency way before. That was the time period when graffiti artist Michael Stewart was beaten to death by police, and Eleanor Bumpurs, sixty-nine years old, was blown away by Officer Sullivan over an eviction with his shotgun. When we were doing the protests and police brutality hearings, I organized a chronology. The reason I knew I needed a chronology was because of Jack Minnis, a crusty old white guy who headed our research department in SNCC. We had a real serious research department. Jack, before there were any computers, could find research from a stone. He did a chronology of violence and intimidation in Mississippi going back to 1961 that he gave out to all of the press people who came down with all these white volunteers the summer of 1964. What he wants people to understand is that it's not this individual—Bull Connor in Birmingham or Mayor Thompson in Jackson, Mississippi, with his "Thompson tanks" for rounding up activists—it's a systematic white supremacy that is governing everything.

I remember a black reporter from what was then *New York Newsday* called me and he said, "Are you a journalist?" I said, "No, no. I just come out of the Movement." He said this chronology was so important because what he could do then is put what's happening to Eleanor Bumpurs into a pattern of violence. It's not an isolated incident.

Crawling Back into the Memory

What brings me joy is my good friends. For example, an image I have from the end of my time with SNCC: I've come back, and I'm now at Columbia University, and we've just had this really hard meeting up at Peg Leg Bates's estate in Kerhonkson, New York, in December of 1966. So I invited all the black folks to my apartment on 112th Street and Broadway (near Columbia). It was one of those big old apartments. I remember we danced until five a.m., all these SNCC people. It was mainly black, but there were a few white people in there, too. It was during a time when we were kind of separate. I remember Stokely could dance, and Stokely was funny as well as being really, really smart. Stokely did something called the Uncle Willie, a dance that Howard University students used to do. We were all dancing. We're doing the boogaloo. Dancing used to bring me joy.

When I got my new knee recently, the best thing for me was when I could do the boogaloo. I started doing a bop. It was like, "Oh, the knee is working! Hello!" Because sometimes you have to have a way of crawling back into the memory to keep you going. It may not be there right now. You may not even have the circle that you need of people, so you have to call it from your experiences.

My Perspective Is Overview

I really do believe that they need to hear from folks who actually did this Movement. For me, the Movement is SNCC. Not because the whole Movement is SNCC, but because that was my experience. I also have a perspective that is in some ways an overall perspective, because I initially came into the Atlanta office. So my understanding of what SNCC is doing and its amazing tributaries—Friends of SNCC, Campus Friends of SNCC, fundraising, all the field offices—comes through that overview that I get when I first come into the national office. That's my lens. It's not somebody sticking a gun into my mouth as they did with Ivanhoe Donaldson. It's not getting beaten like Joyce and Dorie Ladner.

My perspective is through this overview. I know of the many local leaders, planning and organizing on the ground. They stepped out against all the horrible intimidation from the state power, with no help from the federal government. They knew that to step out was to put themselves and their families at risk, but they stepped out, not only for themselves, but for their communities. They gave protection and succor and nurturing and skills to people like me who came into their communities as young people.

When I got the call about being granted an honorary doctorate from Swarthmore, I was amazed. A black man who was the administrator for the president's office called. He left a message. I was on my way down to Princeton because we were having a meeting of the board of the SNCC Legacy Project. I just screamed into the phone when he told me why he was calling. So I get this degree in May of 2012 in the arts. In the presentation they mentioned *Eyes on the Prize*, working in Lowndes County, I think they mentioned the Freedom Schools too. Drum and Spear Bookstore, and the extended Movement experience with the United Church of Christ Commission for Racial Justice. They mentioned the filmmaking for the History Channel with *Slave Catchers, Slave Resisters*. Although I don't think they mentioned the title of *Slave Catchers*. It's like they're going through all the stuff I did in the Movement. It's kind of like, "This is your life."

The thing is, I compare myself to all these amazing people around me in the Movement. Some were older activists, and some of them were young. When I compare myself to that, that's why I was so amazed they were giving me an honorary degree. I mean, I'm nothing compared to, say, a Dorie Ladner who gets beaten up.

I do have a consistency that I think helps. In terms of contribution, there is a body of work that I could probably point to, but a lot of that has to do with all the people around me who provided a foundation and support that allowed me to do that work. The consistency is in working at different levels for a change within the way this country sees black folks, but also more importantly with the way we see ourselves. It really is about how we change the way we see ourselves and what we black people know we can do to change our situation.

Somebody Needs to Tell Them

In terms of the legacy of the Movement, I think it's important to recognize that we didn't just change things for *black* folks. At the March on Washington in 1963, yes, Dr. King did this amazing speech, but the speech that John Lewis,* then the SNCC chairman, gives is amazing too, even after they forced us to take out some stuff. I was there, but I wasn't on staff yet. The original draft of the SNCC speech says at the beginning, "We cannot support wholeheartedly the administration's civil rights bill, for it is too little and too late." Which was also what the March on Washington was organized to support. It asked, "What is there in this bill to ensure the equality of a maid who earns $5 a week in the home of a family whose income is $100,000 a year?" Now, the SNCC speech doesn't say "a black maid," or "a Negro maid" at that time. It's saying "a maid," because we always understood the connection with income disparity and poor white people.

Now, poor white people may not have understood that connection that we had in the speech, but we understood it. So for example, with affirmative action, we open up the door for lots of different kinds of people. It's not just Latinos and Asian Americans who come in. That Stanford University study of affirmative action found it is white women who most benefited from affirmative action, and I'm thinking, "Well, somebody needs to tell *them!*"

Because it's not just a black thing, it would become less easy for the Supreme Court and other white people to go against it, if they knew it's white women who were benefiting from some of this.

---

*In 1987, John Lewis was elected to Congress.

Now, some of the white people don't want these white women working and becoming CEOs anyway, but still, white women themselves need to know that they are the beneficiaries of this thing that we fought for. We opened the gates. We expanded democracy for a lot of different groups. And it would be helpful if we started teaching it that way so it's not just about the black freedom struggle. It is that, but it's also opening it up for a lot of other people.

Judy Richardson speaking at a Boston King Day celebration, 2014. (Credit: Don Harney)

Kathleen Cleaver speaks at a news conference at New York's Kennedy Airport, October 16, 1971, after she arrived back in the U.S. after two and a half years' exile with her husband, Eldridge Cleaver. (AP Photo)

6

KATHLEEN CLEAVER

Kathleen Cleaver traces her commitment to black liberation to her parents and their circle of friends in Tuskegee, Alabama, where service and fighting for one's rights were expected. In addition, Cleaver's extraordinary life and political analysis were shaped by early experiences living outside the United States.

Cleaver was the first woman to serve on the Central Committee of the Black Panther Party. She and her then-husband Eldridge spent time in exile from the United States in Algeria and Korea, where their children were born. In the Black Panther Party, Cleaver developed communications strategies and outreach to media.

After four years in exile, Cleaver returned to the United States in 1973, and with her husband created the Revolutionary People's Communication Network. In 1981, she enrolled in Yale, graduating summa cum laude in 1984, then went to Yale Law School, where she graduated in 1989. She clerked for federal judge A. Leon Higginbotham and became a law professor.

I interviewed Cleaver at her home in Atlanta. She was caring for her teenage grandchildren, who were visiting from the Sudan. She showed a special kind of tenderness and graciousness.

Several women I interviewed asked me if Cleaver was still radiantly beautiful. The answer is yes. Their comments were indicative of black women wanting to celebrate each other and their survival.

Brought Up in the Movement

Both of my parents were activists in the civil rights struggle before I was born and before they met each other. My mother was the daughter of a minister in Richmond, Virginia. Her father, who was also a minister, was a professor at Virginia Union. She and her sister went to school all year round, and by the time my mother was thirteen she was in college where her father taught. By the time she was sixteen, she had a master's degree in math from the University of Michigan. She met my father while she was studying at the University of Michigan.

My father was born in 1911. So he's of the generation of Thurgood Marshall and Ronald Reagan, that era. He was a professor at a black liberal arts college, Wiley in Texas. He was doing a master's or PhD—doing his graduate work in sociology. He had graduated from Fisk. They met, and they fell in love, and they got married in Texas, where he was teaching. I was born there in 1945, right before the war ended.

When I was born, my father was involved with community organizing around the challenge to the Allwright primary in Texas.* He was what you would now call a civil rights activist. He wasn't an attorney; he was a professor. His field was sociology. But he was doing the organizing, and it was interracial.

Both my parents were participants in the civil rights challenges. My mother was a member of something called the Southern Negro Youth Congress, which James Jackson and some other people started. James Jackson was her classmate and neighbor. He ended up becoming very, very active in the Communist Party. She didn't. She was an activist, but not in the Communist Party, but people she knew were. My father's activism was based in Texas. I don't think they probably had socialist parties in Texas.

---

* *Smith v. Allwright*, a Supreme Court case decided in 1944, overturned segregated party primaries.

My parents were conscious advocates and participants in the Civil Rights Movement before I was born. Shortly after I was born, they moved to Tuskegee. I don't really have any memory of Texas. I do remember arriving in Tuskegee, in a big black Nash on a rainy day. It would've been 1948, I believe. My father went to take over something called the Rural Life Council. He's to teach sociology, but it's also an entity that helps rural black farmers access the benefits of our Agriculture Department, and bring them to the campus to learn better ways of farming.

This is the place where George Washington Carver was. That's the context. So I'm growing up in a family of college-educated black people in a community in Alabama around Tuskegee Institute. We're living in faculty housing. All the neighbors that we have are on the faculty, or in the medical school. There's a VA hospital down the street, there's a hospital on the campus, there's a veterinary medicine school across the street. It's a very sheltered and educated little island that I'm growing up in. But I'm too young to know that it's an island.

We have consciousness of civil rights, because they're so absent. We have highly educated faculty who are not able to vote or register to vote, or live beyond a certain area. There's an awareness in Tuskegee that's probably somewhat atypical for black communities in the 1940s, particularly southern black communities. The community I was in was very aware.

White Supremacy Did Not Have a Chance with My Parents—or Me

I left Tuskegee when my father was hired to work in the International Development Agency. Essentially, he became a foreign service officer and moved to India. His field was community development, so what he was incorporated in was an early project. First it was the Ford Foundation. Then it became something called TCM, the Technical Cooperation Mission of the United States, to provide rural community development to Indian farmers.

That sounds like a good thing, but the purpose is anti-communism. India is not a communist state. China is a communist state. India and China were developing a very close relationship. This upset the United States, which has already got India in its grasp with Pakistan. Pakistan broke away. The population of India is somewhat smaller than it used to be when it was British India. Still, India is huge. India is positioned in the center of Asia. If it made an alliance with China, the United States thought that would be a huge problem. This Technical Cooperation Mission was to show the Indian government how to improve the living conditions of the masses of poor farmers. That was my father's field. That's what he did. Truman's policies were very anti-communist. But that's not my father's interest. His interest is in what he called "the barefoot man," poor people. So we moved from Tuskegee to India. I'm nine years old. My brother is seven.

We go to a country where most of the people are brown, and really brown, not like Alabama. There are color variations, but when you see a crowd of Indians, you see brown people, a sea of brown people. When you see the president and the ministers, they're brown. In New Delhi, which is a famous imperial capital of all kinds of different empires, the British empire, the Mughal empire, and this empire, they have all these amazing palaces, and ancient buildings, and they've got the Taj Mahal. I'm in a country of dark people that's amazing, and I'm not quite out of reading fairy tales. It's like a magical place, but all these people are black, and their culture is so elegant and amazing.

Listen: white supremacy evaporated immediately. As if it had a chance with me anyway, not with my parents. It was gone. There was absolutely no substance whatsoever that could convince me that there was anything superior about whites, or anything superior about white culture. I'm looking at one of the most ancient cultures, and it's extraordinary, and all the people are brown. Boom. It was over with. White supremacy is done, and I'm nine years old. It never comes back.

We lived in India for two years. Then we lived in Manila, Philippines, for two years, another brown country. Not as ancient and overwhelmingly sophisticated as India. The Philippines wasn't an empire. It was part of the United States empire, but not like a massive Mughal empire, Persian empire. There are very few places that had that antiquity that are still countries.

In the Philippines, we went to something that was called The American School. It was actually twenty-six nationalities. As I'm growing up, I'm being exposed to all kinds of different peoples, different cultures, different languages, different religions. That's the norm. They have different religions in India. They have different religions in the Philippines. They have all these different languages, different cultures. I'm not being socialized to think white supremacy has any validity, or to think white people are better, or that they're superior or anything like that.

My brother got very ill, so we had to leave the Philippines. We came back, and then he passed away. He had leukemia. My father's next assignment was in Africa, but we didn't know exactly where he was going to go, so my mother and I stayed in America with her family in Baltimore. This was the first time I get to go to an American school that's integrated. They had just integrated the school I went to that year, which I think was '59.

In Baltimore, most of the schools were on a different system. They had elementary, and then they had junior high, and junior high included ninth grade. Then you started high school in tenth grade. But I had just finished eighth grade. I don't want to go to the junior high, so I had to find a school. It's like all these kids that came out of Catholic school were looking for the same thing, a school that starts at ninth grade. There was one, and I went to that. It was very integrated. There were these black kids that had gone to

Catholic school that were in my class. Then these white kids who lived in that area, called Edmondson. I was in an American school with a white teacher, and mixed kids. It was all kind of new to me, actually.

I think I got some really high scores on some tests that they never told me about. I found the records years later and said, "What kind of test is this? What kind of score is this?" IQ scores. No one told me. My parents knew I was very smart. I don't know. They probably did know. They probably didn't think it made any difference to tell me. My mother was a prodigy, so my father said he thought I was going to be in college at sixteen like my mother. No. At sixteen, I was still in high school.

My father was then assigned to Liberia, but by the time he got the assignment, I had already started school, so the next year, we went to live in Liberia, one of Tubman's administrations. While we lived in Liberia, in my second year of high school, I did a correspondence course, taking classes at home. They would send me the lessons and the readings, and I would do them, and write them, and mail them in. They would give me grades.

Then the next year, we went to Sierra Leone. Sierra Leone is a very pretty area. It looks like—which I didn't know then—a West Indian island. Lots of palm trees, and a beautiful beach, very pleasant. I made friends, and had a sheltered life.

Somehow or other, I didn't continue the correspondence course. The school system in Sierra Leone was British, and I just didn't go to school. My father must have left Liberia, come back, gone to Sierra Leone, and that particular year, I didn't go to school at all, which I thought was very fun. I had skipped a grade, so I was a year ahead. I didn't mind it at all.

This is 1961, I guess, so African independence was beginning. My peers, kids my age in Africa, would be talking about movements and independence. "What's wrong with you? You let people walk all over you?" They didn't have much respect for blacks in the United

States because they're too subordinate. I'd listen to this, and I'd hear this, and I'd see. I remember we were in Sierra Leone when it became independent.

Tuskegee, Alabama

My association with America is Tuskegee. It's Alabama. Every time we'd leave the country, we'd come back to Alabama, our home. The only part of the United States that I'm in touch with is Alabama, and the Civil Rights Movement is already under way. It was under way before I left. We left in '54, so the Montgomery bus boycott would've started while we were gone, but it was under way when we came back. It's the same community, so when we come back is when we deal with the boycotts for voting. My father was an activist, and my mother was, so the conversations we'd hear, the things they'd talk about, there was no way I would not have been drawn to the Civil Rights Movement.

I was brought up to be in that movement. There wasn't a time in which these ideas of human rights and social justice weren't being advocated, or implemented, or talked about in my family. I tell my students, "Oh, when they started the boycotts in Tuskegee. I was there. I boycotted." When the Alabama State Legislature passed this statute that changed the boundary of Tuskegee to exclude all the blacks who could have—potentially, if the laws changed—registered to vote. They wanted to make sure that there would be no black vote, so they rearranged the boundaries of Tuskegee. That's the *Gomillion v. Lightfoot* case. The Tuskegee Civic Association, TCA, was very similar to the MIA, Montgomery Improvement Association. They collaborated. Tuskegee was in the county where Rosa Parks was born. So this is kind of the heartland of civil rights activism of the twentieth century. Black people organized a four-year boycott of the merchants in Tuskegee starting in 1957. We said, "Well, if you exclude us from the city limits so that we can't vote, then we will not purchase anything in any of your stores." They put one hundred stores out of business. Some of them never came back. We're talking little stores. There's a book you could check this in, *Reaping the Whirlwind: The Civil Rights Movement in Tuskegee*, by Robert Jefferson Norrell. I teach it, and I like it very much.

White supremacy was very far-reaching. This was the thinking in Tuskegee, Alabama: these people, eventually, if they get the right to vote, will control the city council. Because they'll have more votes than we do. So we have to make sure they don't get any votes and keep the schools segregated, and that whole thing.

Unlike many places, in Tuskegee the civil rights organization, the Tuskegee Civic Association, was led by a professor of sociology, Charles Gomillion, the plaintiff in *Gomillion v. Lightfoot*. Not a preacher. We didn't have preacher leaders. I mean, there were preachers in Tuskegee, but he was a sociology professor, and many of the people who participated were either members of the faculty or they went to churches there.

For that era and that community, you have a highly educated group of black people challenging the discrimination of being denied the right to vote, and all that other stuff. In fact, the educational level in the institute was probably higher than in the town, the county seat of Tuskegee. And the TCA and the MIA worked hand-in-glove. So the boycott that they had started of the buses helped inspire the boycott in Tuskegee of the stores. We really didn't have any buses. Or police or taxis or paved streets. It was a very small community. I would not call it rural, but maybe some people would.

These are my parents' friends and colleagues who were organizing the boycott, and my friends' and classmates' parents who were participating. It wasn't a question of "are we going to do it?" This is what we were doing. There were professors, nurses, doctors, and community people. They were challenging segregation in a very orderly, consistent, intelligent way with these mass meetings.

I Wanted to Be in the Movement

I'd gone to a very sophisticated elementary school—now I realize, looking back, it was started by Booker T. Washington—called Children's House. It was part of Tuskegee Institute. That was my early education. Then I go live in India, and the Philippines, very untraditional elementary education. Come back to the United States briefly. Go to high school one year in Baltimore. Go back. Live with my parents in Africa. One year correspondence course. One year I'm out of school. They had decided I should be in a boarding school. I said, "The only boarding school I'll go to is the one my friend Kay went to." Many people from Tuskegee went to boarding school, so I interviewed them, and they all hated it except for Kay. She said, "We had a ball." I said, "I want to go to this school."

We went up for an interview to George School, and the school was full. I said, "I'm not applying to any other. This is it." Every other school I'd heard about, people told me it was awful, and they didn't like it, so why in the world would I go? My parents had to go to Sierra Leone, so I went with them. Then I was able to come back the following year and become a high school junior. I get there, and it happened to be the high school Julian Bond graduated from. I think when he went there, there were probably two black students. When I went there, Alfred Anderson was another black person from Tuskegee. You ever heard of the Tuskegee Airmen? Chief Anderson was their commander in Tuskegee. His son, Alfred, who most people would've thought was white, was a student at George School. And me, and who else? A townie, a girl who lived in Newtown, and an African exchange student from Uganda. That's the entire black student population of my class. It was a very white environment, and I found it very alien.

It was excellent in terms of education. Because we had something called workshop. Part of your graduation was that you could participate in workshops, community workshops. That means going into Philadelphia and doing some project they've assigned you to that's helping the community. The particular one I ended up in, we painted houses, and we visited the court. This was a Quaker school. They're into social justice in some sense. Nonviolence. Not as much as I thought they were.

Anyway, when I say not as much as I thought they were, I gave a talk in support of the protests in Albany, Georgia, that many young women were actually involved in. It was in the papers in Philadelphia. The picture in the paper was of three young women in the back of a paddy wagon going to jail singing. I was so intrigued. I thought, "Oh my god. They're doing this, and they're singing." It looked like they were having a great time, and it was startling. They're girls. They're in a paddy wagon, and they're happy. That sense of the joy of protest. I wanted to know more about this.

There was a debate going on at my campus about whether it was a good thing or bad thing, so I wanted to take a position. I went back to Philadelphia to one of the places we'd been taken to for work camp to get somebody to tell me all about nonviolent protest, and came back to my school, and gave a speech about why they had to support it. That was the year I graduated. It was '63, right around the time of the Birmingham protests.

How did I get to be a leader? I was trained from the time I was three years old, in a community in which the challenge to segregation was very alive. My father was very much a part of it, and my mother was very much a part of it, all before I was born. And then he goes to the foreign service, and I go out of the United States, so I'm totally moved from any socialization tips except this reaction to racism that my parents would have done anyway.

The whole society I'm in doesn't accept it, so I'm not socialized to accept segregation. I'm not socialized to accept white supremacy. In fact I'm socialized to repudiate it. By 1961 we're living in Sierra Leone, and Sierra Leone becomes independent. The same year, Lumumba was assassinated in the Congo. The whole idea of colonialism and white supremacy is being challenged very, very vigorously.

Within five years there's going to be the Vietnam War and a Black Power Movement, and I'm in high school. So that's when I come back, I go to a Quaker boarding school, and the year I'm graduating is the year of Birmingham. Riots, protests, and the year before was the Albany movement, and the summer is the March on Washington. This is my environment.

This is what I'm drawn to, and this is what's going on right around us, and there's no barrier to my participation. I had an orientation to support the Movement basically from the way I was brought up. I would never have been against it, but I didn't only support it, I wanted to be in it. That's the only thing I cared about doing. I didn't want to be a doctor. I didn't want to be a lawyer. I wanted to be in the Civil Rights Movement. That was my goal.

That was why I was so excited when I went to New York and met someone in SNCC and he said, "What are you doing?" I said, "I'm looking for a job." He said, "Well, I'm looking for a secretary, come down here and apply." I've been wanting to be in SNCC for some time, so I just go in right then.

SNCC

When I came into SNCC in the summer of '66, I was a student at Barnard. I met a group of people who were in SNCC through my boyfriend, Ernest, who had been a veterinary medicine student at Tuskegee and got kicked out for stuff he wrote in the newsletter he started on campus called *Black Thesis*. He was working as a research assistant for a professor at NYU. He had become involved with SNCC in Atlanta, collaborating with his best friend, George Ware. George was a Tuskegee student who had been very engaged in the SNCC projects in Tuskegee, and then he got a master's degree in chemistry and was working in a chemical company called Hoffman-LaRoche in New Jersey.

George and Ernest just so happened to get an apartment at Columbia. I spent a lot of time at their apartment, and I met all these SNCC people that would come through. I met Ivanhoe Donaldson, who had just come up from working as a field secretary in Mississippi, at a party right at the end of the school year. Ernest had gone to Michigan State with Ivanhoe and played football. He and Ivanhoe knew each other.

The New York SNCC office had just replaced the previous director with Ivanhoe Donaldson. They were changing over the leadership in New York to people who were black power–oriented. The emphasis on interracial cooperation was waning, and the focus on black consciousness, black awareness, and black power was ascending. That wasn't true of everywhere in SNCC, but it was in New York where I joined.

Ivanhoe said, "What are you doing?" I said, "I'm looking for a job for the summer." He said, "I'm looking for a secretary. Why don't you come to my office for an interview?" He gave me the SNCC office address, and I joined in June of '66. Stokely Carmichael was the chairman, and it was about two weeks after he made this call for black power. I got included into the SNCC family and began working there. The rest is history. I was plugged in to the Black Power Movement, immediately at its heart. Ivanhoe was one of Stokely's right-hand men. I met Stokely. I met them all. It wasn't that big of an organization any longer.

The New York office was administrative. It wasn't a project. There was no New York project where they're trying to change, like in Mississippi. The Mississippi office would be a project. The Atlanta SNCC office in Atlanta was the headquarters of this organization, and the New York office was really a fundraising office. It provides money for the organization. Why? Because a lot of people who have money organize events in New York. There was a woman who did the mailing lists, a woman named Bobbie Jones who organized parties, a sister, Shirley Belafonte, who helped organize people together, celebrities. There were the parents of Goodman and Schwerner, one of whom was very active. I met the lawyers.

New York was the place all the SNCC people would go for what they call "R and R." If you're tired, you get to go up to New York, or if you need to see a doctor, or you need to see a dentist, you go up to New York and get medical treatment free. Some people were just coming up to New York because they were burnt out. Judy Richardson came back to finish college.

In that particular space, I saw all kinds of people who came through SNCC, who came to New York and stopped by. One story is really funny, I thought. Did you know Joanne Grant? She wrote the book about Ella Baker. She's passed away. She came into the office one day when I had just been hired, and I'm sitting there in the front office. Have you seen a picture of her? Joanne basically has light skin, light brown hair. Maybe she has brown eyes, but Joanne is very racially ambiguous looking. One of her friends—maybe it was her husband—said they went to some hotel in Montgomery that was segregated, and they just checked in. Her husband was white. He said, "Blacks weren't allowed, but it was just Joanne." It is funny. They might not notice. What's funny is that Joanne said— she told me this many years later—that she came into the SNCC office and saw me sitting there at the front. This is two months maybe after black power. She said, "What's that white girl doing in the SNCC office?" She didn't tell me that for many years later. That was before I cut my hair in Afro.

When I got to work in the New York SNCC office, it was fabulous. It was wonderful. I had been trying to do this for years. I know there were hundreds of people just like me. They wanted to be in the Movement. They just couldn't access it. They couldn't be in the place where they could meet the people, where they could get to do it, but they thought it was cool, and they wanted to do it. Particularly women, after Stokely became the chairman. Lord have mercy. The women showed up from everywhere, all over, running to be in SNCC, to be Stokely's girlfriend. I wasn't trying to be Stokely's girlfriend.

My Real Education Was in the Movement

The summer I quit Barnard, I hadn't been going to school all year. I had been living in New York and going to demonstrations and lectures and hanging out with my boyfriend. And I learned how to play chess and played chess. When it came time for exams, I said, "Well, I haven't studied all year. I don't know what good it would do now." Took my exams, and my grades weren't all that different from how they had been the year when I studied. I said, "This school is a waste of time." So I told my father he should not pay any money for me to go to Barnard; it's a waste of money. He should pay me the money, and I will go get a real education in SNCC. And he said, "Okay."

I would not have thought of myself as headstrong. I was focused. But my parents knew, yeah, she gets something in her mind, she wants to go do it. They didn't restrain me from being headstrong. Kind of like, "Okay, well, let's just see how this is going to work out." I think it's also my mother. My mother was very, very mature. She was twenty-six when she married. So most women who had children in the forties were not twenty-six years old with master's degrees in math. That's the atypical mother, particularly atypical black mother. She also did not believe in any corporal punishment. So her views and my father's views were a little different, but he let her views predominate.

I had a, you might say, progressive upbringing. Not really that progressive, but progressive in the sense of allowing me to make choices and to stay out of school and to join the Movement without any downsides. This is my proposal: I said, "You should give me the money you pay Barnard for tuition, and I'll go in the Movement and I'll learn something for real." He said, "Okay, we'll do it for a year."

So I got a check, I think one hundred dollars a month, every month for whatever the length of time the school year would have been.

So at the end of the time, guess it must have been July 1967, he said, "Okay, it's time for you to prepare to go back to college. This is our agreement, you wanted to be out for a year, you have to go back." I said, "Go back to college? I'm in the midst of a revolution; I can't go back to college." And he said, "Well, I can't send you any more money. That was the deal." So I said, "Fine."

The Black Power Movement

My real participation in SNCC as a movement was after I left New York and went down to the headquarters in Atlanta. I was assigned to the campus program. Before my time, they used to call them campus travelers. These were people who would go around to the various black colleges, talk about SNCC, recruit people to work in SNCC, raise money, change the consciousness, et cetera. Our job was to go back onto campuses and educate and recruit students to re-form the base of the Civil Rights Movement that SNCC had been when they were students. SNCC people had come off the campuses into the Movement, so all these people were moving on.

Once SNCC is black power, it's a whole different kind of dynamic, because it's easier to raise money for an interracial group. The previous slogan was "We shall overcome, black and white together." When I came in, it was "black power." That was a little hard on the fundraising. Then when they found that some people in SNCC had published some revealing documents about the way the Israeli military treated Palestinians, and the horrible things they'd done to children, the Jewish base of the funding in SNCC retaliated.

All this happened before I came to Atlanta, so they were basically losing all their money and being shrunk, and turning into a black militant movement. I thought that was great. I'm what, twenty-one?

I just came down from New York. I'm in the very early days of the Black Power Movement. It's extremely exciting. It was exhilarating, as a matter of fact, although there wasn't any money in it.

George Ware had been a leader of TIAL, Tuskegee Institute Advancement League, which was a black student group that participated in civil rights protests along with SNCC. Sammy Younge was one of the activists in SNCC, and Sammy Younge was somebody I grew up with. Sammy was working on this project that George was essentially in charge of, a SNCC voter registration project. Sammy was actually a veteran. He'd been in the Navy, but he'd come back and gone to college in Tuskegee, his hometown. Now, there had been a whole lot of death threats on him because he was very active, and he was reckless in certain ways. Sammy could pass for white, so he liked to do things he could get away with. At times he'd pretend he was white and do things, but sometimes he'd just go in the face of white people. He didn't bite his tongue. He was fun-loving. He was bold. He was driving these white people in Tuskegee crazy. In January 1966, he got shot in the back at a gas station where he had a dispute with the attendant as to which bathroom he was going to use.

That's just the context. They were gunning for him because he was doing all this voter registration and challenging this whole issue of the black majority. Macon County is 80-plus percent black, and Tuskegee is the county seat. If you have even a fraction of the blacks registered to vote, they would overwhelm whatever the whites wanted to do. The issue is so intense. He'd gone to Mississippi and seen what they did with the Mississippi Freedom Democratic Party. He'd come back. He was working with the Lowndes County Black Panther Party,* and he was just really very dynamic.

---

*The Lowndes County Black Panther Party, also known as the Lowndes County Freedom Organization, was an independent black political party formed with assistance from SNCC in central Alabama in 1965 to cultivate and support black candidates for local political offices. Huey Newton and Bobby Seale later adopted the panther symbol for their organization.

When Sammy was killed, George was in New York. I was in New York. His buddy Ernest, who's also from Tuskegee, is in New York. Sammy and me and Ernest are all from Tuskegee. George is from somewhere else in Alabama, and he was a student at Tuskegee. So, Sammy got killed because of the Movement, and George kind of sensed that in some sense he had to do something because Sammy had been working under him. He didn't get Sammy killed, but in December of '66 he came to the conclusion that he had to get back in the Movement. He said, "I'm sitting up here making money working for Hoffman-LaRoche, and people are getting killed." So he left New York and went back to SNCC.

I ended up going to Atlanta and working in the campus program George directed. We hosted a conference at Fisk called Liberation Will Come from a Black Thing, and I was sending out the invitations. March of 1967. We'd invited LeRoi Jones (Amiri Baraka) and other well-known writers we thought would be inspiring. It just so happened that when the conference actually happened, there was a blizzard, and all the East Coast airports were shut, but Eldridge Cleaver, who was also invited, came from the West Coast. He was the only speaker at our conference. That's how he and I met. I'd come to Atlanta in January, and I met him in March. Then he wanted me to come visit him in California. I said, "I have to finish my projects here that I'm working on."

The reason I took a leadership role in the Black Panther Party is because at the beginning of that movement, there were maybe five people. The organization began as the Black Panther Party for Self-Defense, which was created in October of 1966 by Bobby Seale and Huey Newton. The first person to join was a young teenager named Bobby Hutton. It starts out with three. In October 1966, there are three people in the Black Panther Party.

Eldridge and I met at a conference hosted by SNCC's Campus Program at Fisk over the Easter weekend of 1967. And that July I had gone out to San Francisco to visit him and met all the Black Panthers. We had fallen in love and got engaged.

When Huey Newton got shot in October, Eldridge asked me to come back to California and work with the Panthers. He said, "I want you to come out here and work with us." I said, "I don't have any way of getting out there." He never sent me money to get a ticket, and I didn't have any money because SNCC didn't have any money to pay us. But they filed tax returns, so we got a tax refund on the salary that we never got.

Back in Atlanta, a fire was set in the apartment I shared with another SNCC worker, Fay Bellamy. We felt it may have been retaliation for her radio broadcasts, since SNCC was advocating Black Power. They set a fire in a closet where I had just unpacked my suitcase and hung my clothes in, so most of my clothes got burned up. So I told my father I didn't have any clothes, and I think he sent me a check of some amount, I don't know what it was. It was not a large amount of money. Maybe it was $140. Me and my $140 check went to California. I got a ride with a Fisk student and professor I knew from Nashville to Los Angeles. Then I bought a one-way plane ticket from Los Angeles to San Francisco for $12.

I saw Eldridge, and I met the Panthers who I had seen in the summer when I'd been out there. I'd met Huey, and Bobby, and Emory, and the inner circle of Panthers that he hung out with during that summer.

The Black Panther Party that I encountered when I came back in October was Eldridge, Emory, Reggie Forte, and Sherman Forte. Bobby Hutton, a teenager. Emory was a young artist. Eldridge was an ex-convict on parole, and he's not supposed to be associating with any organization that's armed, so he's underground. He's the minister of information of the Black Panther Party. The organization's letterhead did not mention his name, but listed the position as "underground."

On May 2, there was a demonstration in Sacramento challenging the Mulford Act.* The people who were arrested didn't go to trial. They had negotiated a deal that allowed certain people just to go to jail, and made sure Eldridge wasn't among those people. Part of the reason they structured a deal was so he wouldn't be charged. Eldridge had been at the demonstration wearing a black leather jacket and a black beret. But he's an ex-convict. He had no business being there with a group that was carrying weapons but they were able to prove with television footage that he was there as a reporter carrying a camera. I had no role. This was May of 1967. I was in the New York SNCC office, so by the time I meet Eldridge, I am in the Movement.

How did I get to be a leader? I was there.

I was an adult. I was twenty-two. I could write. I could do communication. I understood the problem. I agreed with them. Who else was there? That's what I'm saying. They were in jail. The Panthers, Bobby Seale, most of the people who'd been in the party, were in jail. Huey was in jail. He just got shot in the stomach. Money had gone. They didn't have a Panther office. The party was essentially in collapse. That's how I got to be a leader. I was there.

I was also prepared. There could have been another woman in the room at the meeting. Eldridge could've had another girlfriend there, but he didn't. I was the one that was there. I was the one he picked out. One of his friends said, "No, after he met Kathleen, only Kathleen. She was the only one." He said, "We're trying to figure out what is it about Kathleen? Why is he crazy about Kathleen?"

Do you know who Marvin X is? Marvin X was a poet in the Black Arts Movement, and he came into the prisons to teach prisoners, and he and Eldridge met. Later on when Eldridge got out, Marvin X and some other artists and Eldridge created something called

---

*On May 2, 1967, a group of Panthers assembled with firearms in the California State House to protest the Mulford Act, a bill removing open carry rights in the state of California.

Black House, which was a cultural center in San Francisco. They had Amiri Baraka come and different people. They had plays.

That's how Eldridge was identified when the Panthers met him. Then the Panthers started coming to the Black House. Eldridge got much more interested in the Panthers than in playwrights and painters. The Black House folded, but he had leadership qualities. He'd been a leader in the Nation of Islam in prison. When the Nation of Islam expelled Malcolm X, he quit. The problem was he had filed as a minister in the San Quentin mosque. He had filed a lawsuit for religious freedom for the Muslims, but since the Muslims had expelled Malcolm, he got out. They didn't like that.

Anyway, Eldridge was a person who was a leader. He was also a person who was on parole on special study and had to meet with his parole officer every week. He couldn't actually really be an overt Black Panther leader, but he and I were married, so we did a lot of things together.

We Were Fighters

If I had to characterize my leadership, first of all it's radical, and secondly it was collaborative. I modeled what I did on what I saw Julian Bond do. My area was communication. To put out to the media, the press, the public what the organization is doing and put it out in a way that helps you gain support, protect your movement from police retaliation. That was a large part of what press coverage was about, particularly in the South. If you have cameras, and you have news media who will write about your activity, you may be less likely to be attacked. Or you may less likely be attacked during the day, anyway. So it was a protective thing, but it was also a recruiting thing. You want people to understand what you're doing, so you want to bring them into the Movement. That's how I saw what I was doing.

I made myself communication secretary, nobody else did. They didn't have a communications secretary. They had a chairman, minister of defense, and a treasurer. That's what the Black Panther Party started with. Then they added on minister of information—who was underground, that was Eldridge. Then later on they added on the artist, Emory. He became minister of culture, but he was an artist before, a revolutionary artist. Then they had Field Marshal Don Cox. Field marshal was more of a military thing. Later on they made Stokely Carmichael honorary chair and Rap Brown honorary minister of justice. So the leadership structure expanded and changed as the Movement grew.

You have a conceptual structure that's called leadership. We in the Black Panther Party, our structure was not leadership. Our structure was revolutionary. We were trying to make ourselves revolutionaries. What does a revolutionary do, how do you get the consciousness of a revolutionary? This is how we were functioning.

Huey was shot in '67 in October, a few days after Che Guevara was murdered in Bolivia. That phase was during the Vietnam War. He was shot, but he wasn't killed. It was a shoot-out with the police. It was an extraordinary moment because in '64, '65, '66, '67 you keep seeing these riots, rebellions, uprisings. What are they provoked by? Policeman shooting a black guy. Usually a young man. In Newark, it was a twelve-year-old. I'll never forget. There's pictures in *Time* magazine, *Newsweek* magazine, the cover of this little boy lying on the ground. The people tore up Newark.

Then there's Detroit, or "Destroyt." The images were smoke in the background, troops under the tents. That was the 101st Airborne, that Commander Westmoreland from Vietnam had previously commanded. The U.S. Army is in Detroit. Geronimo Ji-Jaga, who later became a Panther in Southern California, is in the army unit deployed to Detroit at that time. He said he and other black soldiers were helping the brothers on the roof, telling them where the armory was and how to get guns and how to keep this going. For which they all got punished with a second tour of duty in Vietnam. This is the context into which I am put as I go to California. I go out there in July of '67, so it's in the context of all these uprisings and rebellions. So we are thinking there's a revolution that's going to take off. How do we build our revolution? How do we create our organization, how do we become revolutionaries? Leadership is a very civilian concept. It's not only used by civilians, but it's a civilian concept, and that's not what we were. We saw ourselves as fighters.

I'm trying to explain the Black Panther Party when I came not as a visitor, but as a participant. When I came as a visitor they had an office. Bobby was the chair, Huey was a minister of defense, Eldridge was underground. He lived in San Francisco; all their activity was over in Oakland. He was not supposed to associate with them, so it was all kind of covert. But they would hang out together and they would come over to his apartment, and he went over to Oakland. At one point, he was banned from leaving the San Francisco Bay area by his parole authorities. It probably had to do with being arrested in Sacramento.

We were in a moment that we thought of as a revolutionary moment. We're at the beginning of something, and we were focused on how to be a revolutionary. If you become a revolutionary in a vanguardist revolution, by definition you're going to be in a structure that's giving leadership to a movement.

So we had a leader, Huey Newton. He got shot. We had a leader, Bobby Seale. He was in jail. Well, next one down the line is Eldridge Cleaver, he's a minister of information, and he's actually a very competent leader, but he's on parole, and he cannot be seen as leader of an armed organization. But I think by the time Huey got shot in October the law had been changed, so the Panthers were not openly carrying guns then. It was very tricky. Eldridge spoke at a rally in which Coretta Scott King spoke in April of '67. It was a rally of people, an anti-war rally at Kezar Stadium, and he introduced himself as a leader of the Black House, which had a community as a cultural group.

Revolutionaries are not interested in the normal operating of society. A revolutionary is the one that transforms that. The way in which they do it is by creating revolutionary movements, revolutionary concepts, revolutionary ideas.

You have to build up a revolution to the point where it has enough substance for there to be leaders. We had so-called civil rights leaders, but they were products of a grassroots movement that they didn't lead. But people outside of the Movement think, "Oh yes, King was the leader."

Martin Luther King was twenty-six years old, had just done his theology doctorate up in Boston. His first job is the pastor of Dexter Avenue Baptist Church. How did he become so-called leader of the Montgomery Bus Boycott?

There's two competing figures in Montgomery. One of them is E. D. Nixon, who's a union organizer from the Brotherhood of Sleeping Car Porters. He's an organizer and a leader. The other one was Coach Lewis, who was at Alabama State. So, they are both known political black men leaders in Montgomery. When the Alabama attorney general and the Montgomery County Circuit Court prohibit the NAACP from functioning, how do they do that? They demand to have all the records of the leadership, of the members. And the NAACP isn't going to do it, the court issues a huge fine and ousts the organization from the state, so forth and so on, and so then they just don't have any members in the NAACP.

They create the MIA, Montgomery Improvement Association, which most of the people in NAACP are participants in. Now they have to come up with a leader for the MIA. King was the compromise. They don't want to either choose Nixon and have Coach Lewis mad or choose Coach Lewis and have Nixon mad, so they picked somebody else who's fresh and new. Not Rosa Parks, but her buddy Johnnie Carr said they just loved King's big words and his eloquence, and he's twenty-six years old. Johnnie Carr and Rosa Parks had gone to school together. She came and gave a talk I heard. She said "Oh, he was something. He was inspiring." So they picked King. They're picking him. What I'm saying is the people who are picking him are the leaders. This is what I'm trying to get at.

On Liberation

There's different ways in which movements function as opposed to a military, a corporation, a government. The kind of leadership notions that most people have come from corporate structures. Military, states, corporations. Social justice activism does not use that structure, and social justice activism doesn't use the kind of people who are leaders in those contexts. Leadership is not a viable concept in the context of a revolution. Which means that when you say "leadership" that's all nice, well, and good, but civil rights are the rights of citizens, so if you're a citizen you have these rights. So that was that whole dynamic. We are second-class citizens, but we're not really citizens like the other people. So therefore we want to get our civil rights.

It's kind of old-fashioned. I mean 1940s, 1950s. By the sixties we were calling for liberation. By the time I met Eldridge at a SNCC conference, the conference we had organized was called *Liberation Will Come from a Black Thing*, so it was post–Black Power. This is different. That means we are acknowledging that lack of rights is a form of imperial power or community domination. We were using concepts that were produced by the post–World War II revolution for independence and self-determination in the colonial world. When I was a little kid, the world map was all pink for Britain or green for France. But from '45 on, from the day I'm born, countries are becoming independent. India becomes independent, Indochina (now Southeast Asia) becomes independent, this one becomes independent, Algeria becomes independent, so this escalates.

The old nineteenth-century imperial world is deteriorating and being replaced with a different world. The Vietnam War is right in the crux of all of this. The Vietnam War, I call it proxy war, Soviets versus United States. The communist world fighting the capitalist world. Although they all want to say it's about freedom. That's a time in which our movement escalated, and it went from civil rights to black power very quickly and from black power to black liberation. That's a period of revolutionary change that very few people in this country anticipated. Americans don't anticipate revolution, they seek stability. Don't have it, but they seek it.

For the people who went into the Black Power Movement, most of them were brought up Christians, but by the time they get in that movement they're focused on something else other than faith. They're focused on radically altering the relationship between the larger society and the oppressed people. When I got there, it was really focusing on what we call black consciousness. Black is beautiful, black power, black arts, black liberation. We were moving out of nineteenth-century concepts into a more modern way of thinking, but we were bound by these nineteenth-century concepts. Because that's what all this stuff basically is, you know. I love Du Bois's comment. He said in the nineteenth century, everything good, everything powerful, everything beautiful is considered white.

Race is full of pretension. It's all this pretending, but then they believe it. They start believing what they pretend. You can't go dig race up in the ground—you can find roots, and you can find rocks, and you can find dirt. You can go up in the moon and you can find dirt and rocks, but you can't find any race. You can't find it. You can't touch it. It's conceptual, that's what I mean. They've attached that concept, because it didn't always exist. It's not a real thing, it's a conceptual thing, but you can't tell Americans that.

When we talk about Black Power, we're challenging that whole white European imperial power structure that America came out of and fed back into and became the dominant imperial power. Commercially, not with owning property like Britain, but owning control, and then militarily. It now is the supreme military power in the universe. That's very disturbing, because the people in charge are not smart. If they were, we'd have a better society. Enormous number of smart people in America, but they don't seem to be able to take control, you know?

Kathleen Cleaver at the Black Panthers reunion, Yale University, in New Haven, Connecticut, on April 3, 2002. (Credit: AP Photo / Steve Miller)

Gay McDougall with Nelson Mandela in 1994 as he votes for the first time.
(Courtesy of Gay McDougall)

7

GAY McDOUGALL

Born in 1947, McDougall has a lifelong commitment to civil and human rights that began early. In her teenage years, she was selected to become the first African American to integrate Agnes Scott College in Decatur, Georgia. During her two years there, she was the *only* black student at this all-girls college just outside Atlanta. She transferred to Bennington College, where she earned her undergraduate degree. She is a graduate of Yale Law School and the London School of Economics.

After the Civil Rights Movement, McDougall forged a storied career in international human rights. She was the executive director of global rights for Partners for Justice and became the first United Nations expert on minority issues. McDougall was instrumental in the Free South Africa Movement's protests against apartheid from 1980 to 1994, organizing demonstrations and support groups for this cause. At the same time, she served as director of the Southern Africa Project of the Lawyers' Committee for Civil Rights Under Law. In that capacity, she worked with South African lawyers—often under secrecy to protect their safety—to gain the release of thousands of political prisoners.

As apartheid was ending, she was named one of five international members of the South African governmental body established through the multiparty negotiations to set policy and to administer the country's first democratic, nonracial elections in 1994. The result was the election of President Nelson Mandela and the transition from apartheid.

When Nelson Mandela died, pictures captured McDougall at his side as he cast his first vote as a free South African in April 1994. In 1998, McDougall was the first American to be elected to oversee the United Nations International Convention on the Elimination of All Forms of Racial Discrimination. In 1999, she was recognized with a MacArthur Foundation Fellowship, often cited as a "genius award," for her human rights work. Most recently, McDougall was a distinguished visiting professor at Fordham Law School's Leitner Center for International Law and Justice and is a member of the faculty of the Oxford University Masters of International Human Rights Law Programme. She has received honorary doctor of law degrees from six universities including Georgetown University Law Center and the University of the Witwatersrand (South Africa). In 2015, the government of South Africa bestowed on her its national medal of honor for non-citizens, the Order of O.R. Tambo Award, for her extraordinary contributions to ending apartheid.

Then, as now, a woman whose delicate physical appearance belies a steely will and steadfast dedication to the liberation of all oppressed peoples, she is a visionary with a restless imagination. McDougall worked on civil and human rights issues for many years before meeting and marrying John Payton, another famed civil and human rights attorney. He died in 2012.

I interviewed McDougall in her office at Fordham. Before we discussed leadership, she wanted to talk specifically about the origins of the fight for civil rights in America and to frame the international human rights struggle.

Early Social Justice Consciousness

I grew up in a family where caring about and addressing unfairness were important. I lived in a house where my great-grandfather, a minister, was a presiding elder in the AME church. Doing the right thing had concrete form in my house.

One of my aunts worked as a field organizer for the YWCA in the '40s and '50s, going across the South trying to form interracial clubs among young women—a precursor, really, of the civil rights era. All those things were swirling around me. They were a part of my upbringing. When I was growing up in Atlanta, our community was two steps away from slavery. We'd go to our friends' houses in what we called "the country" because they had horses. In reality, they lived in shacks where the wallpaper was newspaper. They had outhouses. Poverty was everywhere.

Most of the women in my family were social workers. I would sometimes join them on home visits. There was no question that we were in a ghetto. We were aware that other people had better, but our world then was our community. Even as a child, I was very concerned about the poverty around me, but when my aunts took me around I saw our circumstances in a different light. That experience had a powerful impact on me.

We didn't have a television until I was around eight years old. We only read the African American newspaper and, of course, *Jet* magazine. Television quickly brought us a worldview. This was before legal segregation ended in Georgia. I remember the first time I saw the United Nations—on a little black-and-white TV. There were all of these guys—of course they were guys—black men in their ceremonial robes from Africa, looking proud, sitting down next to people from Sweden and other countries. They were all on equal terms and they were there to make decisions. This blew me away. Seeing the UN planted in my mind that there was a larger world that was different from the "Jim Crow" that we lived in. It gave us the hope that fueled our protest against segregation.

In high school, I began to see some other worlds. There was a global movement that came through Atlanta very focused on gaining African American converts. It came to my high school, Washington High. It was the Moral Re-armament Movement. People had to give their personal possessions away and join this movement to re-arm morality. I was really fascinated by the call for personal financial sacrifice and the idea that people would go to other countries to help others.

All of us in the Atlanta Civil Rights Movement did our part. Marching, refusing to ride the buses, walking instead, refusing to shop at white stores—where we were not respected—wearing old clothes instead. We attended church rallies where spirits were buoyed for the marches ahead. Yes, people were scared sometimes, and there were good reasons for fear. I remember one night when the Klan encircled a church we were in, and Martin Luther King was giving a speech to rally the crowd for the next action. The Klan was outside threatening to kill anyone who came out of the church.

Taking My Place in the World

Gender discrimination was everywhere, except at home. My immediate home and my extended family were very women-dominated. Outside of home was different—in churches, schools. Schools had mostly female teachers, but only male administrators. All of the work in the church communities was done by women. My mother was superintendent of the Sunday School at our church, St. Mark's African Methodist Episcopal Church. But the pulpit was a male preserve. That's where I can first remember taking note of the irrationality of patriarchy. Even though I was an adolescent, it was very clear to me that the pastors, the bishops, and the presiding elders were of far less leadership quality than the women who were denied equal status.

The Civil Rights Movement was not an exception, and black women's organizations acknowledged women's leadership roles.

Outside of church, I was not a joiner. I was very reluctant to sign the membership card of any organization, because I did not want to be just another woman whose role was to follow the male leader. I never signed up for women's organizations either. My mother, who went to Spelman College—where sororities were prohibited—made not joining a sorority a matter of principle. My sister and I followed her lead. We wanted to define ourselves as individuals first.

I always swam upstream. I think it is very important to maintain one's intellectual integrity, not to just follow along. That's another lesson from my mother. She was impressed by the writings of Henry David Thoreau, particularly those on civil disobedience and living a life guided by your own drumbeat and principles. Explore the ideas that are different, choose the path not taken by others. Instead of learning French, why not study Russian? So I took five years of Russian-language training in high school. However, she also taught me that certain things are right and there are some things that are just wrong. You must always have a moral compass that guides you though life.

Women in the Movement

For anyone who was close enough to the Movement to see actual preparations going on for protests, marches, and events like the Poor People's Campaign, I think it would be hard to conclude that women weren't playing traditional roles, that is, showing up in large numbers and handling the infrastructure work. Nothing could have happened without the infrastructure work. Most women didn't get recognized or named, largely, unless they were Coretta King. But they—we—were there. Building infrastructure, that's everything. It is the work that builds a movement. Community organizing, passing out flyers, providing food and accommodations, keeping people comfortable, tending to their needs. Singing the songs was also very important. Transporting people to the gathering places. When families came, it was the mother who brought the family, not the father. Women's contributions were substantial.

There were women who eventually emerged as leading figures. Fannie Lou Hamer, even in her time, was celebrated for her contribution. Everybody would say that. But there were so many others. Dorothy Height made sure that she was not ignored. Ella Baker. Emmett Till's mother, Mamie. Rosa Parks. Diane Nash was a shero, and a prominent leader in the Nashville student movement. Angela Davis. Kathleen Cleaver's substantive contributions were not celebrated to the extent they should have been during that time. She is remembered now more for her iconic looks and her connection to Eldridge rather than for her brilliant mind and her hard work on the Panthers' programs to support the black community's social needs. These are all exceptional women and we must take every opportunity to "say their names." And they stand on the shoulders of many others whose names we do not know. But they made tremendous contributions of activism, courage, and thought leadership with little or no public recognition. Most did not seek the recognition, but it still matters that it has remained elusive.

Confronting Sexism

I recently had an argument with this young man who has written a biography of Stokely Carmichael. I took him on about Stokely's sexism, and the author went berserk. "Stokely was a sexist? No, no, no, there's one phrase that everybody knows, he said in jest, as a joke in some situation, and it's just followed him."* I said he'd never taken it back.

You look at the leadership of the West Coast Panthers until you get to Elaine Brown, who finally says to everybody after the Movement is over, "Hey, these guys were so sexist."

---

*Stokely Carmichael, SNCC leader and later Black Power proponent, joked that "the proper position of women in SNCC is prone."

The Anti-Apartheid Movement was also sexist. Being the executive director of the Southern African Project of the Lawyers' Committee, which was my own shop, allowed me to have autonomy and to set the terms for my involvement in specific activities. My organization had unique access to people inside South Africa, which most other U.S.-based anti-apartheid groups did not have. Both the autonomy and the connections inside the country gave me a kind of standing to do my own thing.

When male leaders tell the history of the Anti-Apartheid Movement, I am mostly overlooked. But not only was I there for every important event, I played an important role in every event. I was there on the night we planned the tactic to stage a sit-in at the South African embassy that would result in high-profile arrests. I was there every day for the entire year, rain or shine, in the demonstration lines outside of the embassy and acting as one of the legal counsel representing those who were arrested to get them out of jail. I also staged a Lawyers Against Apartheid Day and organized upwards of a thousand lawyers to march, many of them from corporate law firms with their attaché cases in tow.

At the same time, I was raising millions of dollars from international donors and secretly sending it into South Africa and Namibia to lawyers there to pay for them to defend political prisoners and to file litigation that challenged apartheid structures.

I met my husband, John Payton, the first day I moved to Washington, in 1980. It was love at first sight. We had been called to a meeting hosted by Randall Robinson at TransAfrica. It was a very small group, maybe there were six of us, convened to think about strategies to use in our anti-apartheid activities. We talked about going into the embassy, sitting down, and refusing to leave. Five years later, it was the strategy that really loosened up the political space and gave members of Congress the political will to pass sanctions legislation and to override a veto by President Ronald Reagan. John was very involved already in the things that I thought were important, and he became involved even more. He was the chief lawyer of the Washington

Movement, and did that brilliantly. When the liberation movements named me to be a member on the Electoral Commission that organized and ran the first democratic elections in South Africa in 1994, John came with me for the year I needed to relocate to Johannesburg. He also led a team of monitors that observed the elections in the South African Bantustan Bophuthatswana.

We were companions and each other's closest advisor. The nicest thing John ever said to me was that I was always skipping ahead of his imagination. And, you know, that also showed what our bonds were about, what we gave to each other.

Standing Up to Make the Difference

While in college, I worked for the U.S. Civil Rights Commission in its heyday. I was attached to the office of the General Counsel in the Washington, D.C., headquarters, but I also did field work in Alabama and Texas. That was really fantastic. In those days the commission was bold; it was ready to be out there and lead the charge. Filled with people who had new ideas and worked hard and really wanted to get the job done. As I traveled, going across Alabama and Texas, I saw things I will never forget. We were looking for the human stories about life as African Americans and Mexican Americans living in those southern states during those times. We needed to know what the issues were, find people willing to testify in public. Then we would set up a hearing for presentations to the commissioners. It was an absolutely spectacular job for me at that age. My work on the Civil Rights Commission helped me to decide that I was going to be a lawyer, and that I was going to be a civil and human rights lawyer.

My participation as an African American in the struggle against apartheid was unique. I was involved both here in the United States and in South Africa. I worked in South Africa to free political prisoners, and then later with the multiparty congress on behalf of Mandela's African National Congress party to write the constitution. I was later put on the sixteen-member commission that actually ran the elections, and I was there with Mandela when he voted for the first time. I was also involved in the independence of Namibia. Namibia has a similar but different story.

One of the things that is very important—and it sounds very simple, but it's the starting point—is that all those African freedom movements started from inside their countries. The critical thing is to support the people on the ground, helping them in ways that they need. I was able to surreptitiously bring large amounts of cash into South Africa to pay the lawyers. I also did backup research they could use in their cases. I did the same thing during the constitution-making process. The credit for their independence goes to black South Africans. It's all them, but you can find ways to help. That's the best outcome.

In my life, I've learned that no advancement comes from one person alone. There has to be a number of people, a critical mass, willing to stand up, and sometimes do more than just stand up, to make the difference. There are some skills to leadership, but true leaders do not exist without other people who build the infrastructure. Another observation I have is that most of the groundwork is done by women—and women must learn to demand their recognition.

Recent photograph of Gay McDougall in her office. (Courtesy of Gay McDougall)

Gloria Richardson, head of the Cambridge Nonviolent Action Committee, pushes aside a National Guardsman's bayonet during a demonstration in Cambridge, Maryland, on July 21, 1963. (Credit: AP Photo)

8

GLORIA RICHARDSON

Gloria Richardson had several distinctions in her civil rights involvement. Born in 1922, Gloria Richardson was an older adult during the Civil Rights Movement. She became involved to support her teenage daughter and other youth demonstrators. Unlike the gentle public persona of Rosa Parks or the constrained anger of other women leaders who concealed their rage, Richardson was openly militant, leading street protests and questioning nonviolence as a tactic. She challenged economic inequality with a boycott. Most women leaders were not afforded that title, but *Ebony* magazine called Richardson the Lady General of Civil Rights. Annette Brock writes that under Richardson's leadership, the Cambridge movement became known as "the first grassroots movement outside of the deep South."

Since blacks in Maryland already had the right to vote and the Richardson family was relatively well-off, Richardson's militant leadership was often cited as unexpected; she was considered an unlikely rebel. Brock further writes that during a trial about the demonstrations she led, the judge excoriated her for allegedly disgracing her family name. What the judge failed to acknowledge was that under the surface, her lot was not much different from that of other blacks. Richardson understood that the black middle class was still considered less than first class by the white majority and treated as such. Richardson is in the black radical activist tradition of self-defense and uncompromising positions on equality. Richardson's questioning of nonviolence inspired later efforts of Black Panthers and others who adopted more militant responses to social injustices.

After the successful protests that she led, Richardson married photographer Frank Dandridge, who had covered the Cambridge movement. She moved permanently to New York City and worked in human services. This interview took place at Richardson's apartment near Union Square. Ironically, the television news was showing footage of protests of black youth against police brutality. Richardson characteristically supported the youth and questioned the lack of black social and political progress. Almost ninety-three at the time of our interview, she had not lost her passion for justice or her clarity of analysis.

Growing Up

I was brought up in a household where everybody did some kind of community service. I also grew up about ten minutes away from where Harriet Tubman was active. I grew up with those people as part of the community back then. Cambridge, Maryland, wasn't a place where people were coming in and out. People had been there, the grandparents, the great-grandparents. Whatever their socioeconomic or religious background was, they had been there ever since they were children.

My grandfather came up in the time when the group of men in New York, Philadelphia, and further south were thought of as "race men," were achieving themselves, and they thought it was incumbent upon them to bring everybody else with them and to fight for people's rights. They knew each other, whether you were in Baltimore or a rural area. They wanted everybody to come along.

My grandfather was one of those men, and I grew up in a household like that. Actually, I don't know what we were supposed to be, but my grandfather and father always turned their nose up at middle-class people. My father said they were the ones, the pretend middle class, that would call him up at eleven at night at the drugstore asking him to bring a three-cent stamp by their place. For my grandfather, they weren't trustworthy, but my grandfather also told me, "You could not have the benefits you have today if the people in the community were not patronizing our businesses."

I didn't experience sexism in my family. I didn't see it with my mother and grandmother, and I didn't personally experience it with my uncles or my grandfather or my father. Bernice Reagon says when I came down to Atlanta and other women would complain, she said, "I knew you didn't understand anything we were saying." If I was chastised, it was on some other basis. It wasn't because I'm a woman or girl and I have no business talking back to you, or whatever. The whole family was supportive of my endeavors in the

Movement. It may have been because until I was about seventeen, there were no other grandchildren, male or female. After that, there were two grandchildren that came.

I can remember when I was little, after we moved to Cambridge, we'd take trips up to Baltimore, and my father might say to me, "Here comes the state police car. If he comes up close and passes, don't anybody look at him." And I can remember thinking, "Gee. That's strange." But you know, children were always peeking out at things. So I would sit there and look.

I can also remember that my father couldn't go to the hospital which was close to our part of town. Neither could my uncle when he got typhoid fever. Even though he had graduated from Harvard Law School and was supposedly considered a good citizen.

So, I think there were things like that that happened that maybe you don't really concentrate on at the time, but you internalize it as a child. It wasn't until maybe the fifties, when laws started being passed, that I seriously thought about it. In the first generation we think it's because it's all your own doing. You were smart and did this and did that. After two or three generations, you begin to know: oh, back there then, they did things, and now what are we doing here three generations later? The big thing in America is supposed to be that each generation does better than the last. And then you find out we're still at the same place.

I see now that historically they'd always, for a long time, had a black commissioner for the Second Ward in Cambridge, even before my grandfather served in that position. So, people had gotten loans, paid them off, a lot of things like that that make you comfortable living where you are. I suppose it would still have been like that until *Brown v. Board of Education* and some of those other things started going on.

Joining the Movement

Initially I probably wasn't too aware of what they were doing, but my uncle and cousin provided the bail for protesters during demonstrations against discrimination down Route 50 on the Eastern Shore of Maryland and at Gwynn Oak Park, an amusement park outside of Baltimore that refused to admit blacks. Blacks couldn't use the facilities in the parks. In that process of CORE and NAACP gathering people, they asked for people from the new Student Nonviolent Coordinating Committee to come up to Baltimore.

The governor, J. Millard Tawes at that time, happened to come from Crisfield on the Eastern Shore of Maryland. The demonstrators apparently could not get any decision or involvement from him. So at Christmastime, they followed him to his hometown in Crisfield, which also happens to be where my grandmother came from. Protesting along Route 50, almost all the towns they stopped in, like Salisbury, at least made some attempt to meet with the governor and modify his policy, mainly to keep their stores and their restaurants running smoothly without demonstrations. The power people in town just decided, "We don't want this mess here. So let's agree."

After the Freedom Riders went down to Crisfield, on their way back, my cousin said to them, "You know, where you all really need to go is through Cambridge"—where I lived—"because that's totally shut down." George Kent, who taught high school in Cambridge, had written a dissertation at the University of Maryland saying black people in town were politically apathetic. They dropped off two field secretaries. I didn't go to the first rally, but people of all ages just poured out into the churches, four hundred and five hundred people at a time.

After the SNCC field secretaries interviewed people, they decided that they would call for demonstrations. They had been in town a couple of weeks, I think, and they wanted to find local younger folks that could take them around the town and show them where to go. My uncle sent them to my house. On the weekends, my daughter Donna would make cookies, and eight or nine of her high school friends would be back in the kitchen cooking and carrying on. So I said to the SNCC people, "Well, go back there and ask them. Maybe they'll agree." And they did. So my daughter and friends helped lead those first demonstrations.

For two or three weeks, I really didn't focus on the demonstrations. I just thought, "Oh, that's good that's going on." But then the high school and grammar school students shut the town down. That's when the white folks were scared to go in and out of the stores, even though the students weren't doing anything to them— they were peacefully picketing.

So, the white community's economic structure started crashing, and then the preachers went down and said, "Okay, we'll have peace for a while. Can you all decide what you want to do?" At the time, my cousin, the bail bondsman, was a co-chairman of what later became the Cambridge Nonviolent Action Committee. As people got arrested, he began to feel that was a conflict, and he dropped out. A businessman in town came to me and asked me if I would take my cousin's place, because they thought I, or my family, was economically secure enough that I could be outspoken without risking my livelihood.

So, he came and asked me, and I said, "Yes." I had gone to one or two meetings by that time, and I thought that the young people had done such a fantastic job. One time when I went on a picket line, my daughter had to put me off, because I was trying to trip a white person who was going by the line. She just tapped me. She told me, "Mom, get out of the line." And I did. It was a whole switching relationship.

The parents that had been supporting the kids then got together and said, "Well, SNCC is a student thing, but maybe we all can go down there to the conference, and SNCC will give us permission to start an adult affiliate." So that's what we did, me and my cousin's wife. The community gave us money to go down, and we went to the SNCC conference, and they said, "Yes." So we came back and started.

The Cambridge Movement

When we came back from the SNCC conference, we began to do organizing throughout the county. Initially, SNCC was into voter registration. Going to different neighborhoods within the Second Ward and in the county allowed us to form a basis for what later became the Cambridge Civil Rights Movement.

I didn't think the registration drive would come to much, and it didn't. People came out but once they got elected, they ignored what we wanted. The Cambridge Committee was purely local. The two big SNCC organizers, William Hansen and Reginald Robinson, probably left sometime in the middle of the second year. It was local people that carried the Movement. We met in my father's drugstore. He had died. I had been unable to keep pharmacists there at the time, but I ran it myself for a while, while the white pharmacist's stand could do our prescriptions. Then I had an argument with the black doctor, and he stopped sending people there, so we eventually had to close it down. But that's where we met.

The other thing was no religious affiliation, no club affiliation. I mean, you could do that in your personal life, but not in the Movement. You couldn't be divided because "My club is better than your club," or whatever. No Republicans, Democrats—no politics. You could go out and vote however you wanted, but within the Movement, everybody's on the same team. I think it worked in a lot of ways, because you didn't get those splits in the community along socioeconomic lines. Outside of that, you can go do whatever together—the Baptists, or the Methodists, or the AME Church. Actually, the churches were not that supportive. I thought that maybe they had mortgages and reacted according to that situation.

When we formed the committee, we did it kind of like my grandfather's old political organizing. The committee members were from every section of town, from each of about twelve different sub-neighborhoods, and were people who that neighborhood felt close to and would go to with problems. So the so-called executive board knew the people, and the people knew them. That meant we had a two-way conversation going on. That came out in our meetings, where people shared what they were ready and able to do, or wanted to do. So, there was unity there. I mean, there were a couple of so-called saditty* blacks that stopped speaking to us. But that was okay, because we didn't need them anyhow.

The leadership was a steady group. But also, you gotta understand that SNCC was not structured. So it's not like you had a membership card or whatever. Even in our small committee meetings that we held in my father's drugstore, if somebody up the street wanted to come in and listen, they could, because it wasn't any big secret. They could disagree, or whatever. I think we were lucky, because sometimes we just would meet among ourselves, which usually gave us a Plan A and a Plan B. So if you started out on what the consensus was and it wasn't working, you could switch. And everybody kind of knew that, so it kept us from making really horrible mistakes.

I think my first heads-up that we would need the whole board involved was when we went down to the city council, and one of the men said to me, "Well, why are you here? You don't live in a house that's leaking. You've been to school." I said, "Oh, is that how it is? Well, I'm representing people on our committee that you know who are bringing information from their neighborhoods and who them-

---

*"Saditty" is spelled various ways (seditty, saddidy) but means a person with a superior attitude, often viewed as superficial and self-righteous.

selves have these problems." And they didn't want to hear that. So the next time we went, we just took everybody, ten to twelve people, down there so that at least they would not be able to say, "Well, that's not happening to you."

In early '61, that summer, we did a lot of writing to federal and state agencies—you know, complaints, "We'd like to have this resolved." In the middle of that, we had to come to the city if we were going to meet with any black folks in any agency, because we found out that we would go, have fine conversations and say, "You get back to us by the end of the week." One week, two weeks, three weeks, and we didn't hear from them. So we just decided, well, instead of going, if we don't really know whether they've giving the black agency representatives any power or not, we would just ask.

That's how the Cambridge Nonviolent Action Committee started. Because we weren't involved in politics, our thing was to create enough chaos to attract Washington. Because we were close to Washington, and because the president was running around New York talking about democratic ideals over there.

Eventually, that worked. The white politicians and mayor and the people that controlled them were not gonna give an inch. We then decided that we would do picketing every day, no matter how many or how few people we had, and also larger rallies and marches. By the time Robert Kennedy got involved, I think the first thing he said to me was, "You know that town is broke." And my response was that I really didn't care because we were broke to start out and had been there for generations.

People played different roles. There was a group of young people in high school that did the walkie-talkies. There was a group of men that had to go to Baltimore and Wilmington and Dover, Delaware, for new jobs. That's how we formed our spy network. Because when they got home from work, most of them would go up on this main street, Pine Street, and maybe for an hour talk to the men that were on the street up there.

Mainly, the people that were available in the day were the women. The men's role was to protect the Second Ward as soon as night fell. There were exchanges of gunfire going back and forth when white folks would come out to bomb or shoot and go traipsing through the backyards and stuff. The men in the community were there to stop them. I think the score was nine white folks shot and zero black. These were World War I and II veterans, and they knew what they were doing. They organized themselves, even down to having medical supplies in case anything really got bad. They were pretty well organized, and they fended off most of those people.

The men in town may have fought and been sexist before the Movement and afterwards, but during that time it had gotten so bad they would have to leave their wives home with guns when they went to work at night. So there was a sharing there. Now, that's not to say that the women still didn't iron something or cook a dinner, but it was more equal. I remember when I first started out, I was on the street one night, and the state police were jack-booting down the street: boot, boot, boot, boot. About ten or twelve women turned around and said to the men, "Why're you letting them come down after me? Instead of beating us on Saturday night, go out and beat them." And I thought: "Oh. Oh!" I don't know whether that motivated them, but then the men did start reacting on their own terms.

With Robert Kennedy, I don't think it was the racism that first got him. I think it was the abject poverty that really got him. And that he also knew how they had treated Irish people when they first came here. This was his first hook when we took him the results of our survey against the U.S. Census for that year. We depended on him because when he ran his brother's campaign, he was known for being ruthless. We figured if we could prove to him that what we were saying was true, in terms of our condition, and he got involved, that he could bring to bear whatever they controlled in the federal government.

At whatever point Robert Kennedy got involved, we and other members of the committee had been going back and forth for three or four weeks. The Guard had come in. At that time, in order for us to get from Cambridge to Washington, they had to put police cars up and down the road just to hand us over, because the Klan there was active.

Then the Baltimore Civic Interest Group, the CIG,[*] a group comprised of high school and college students, had to kind of separate from the NAACP, because of what they called "the treaty." During that process, people tried to direct protesters to the NAACP in an attempt to exercise control. They would say, "Well, we're going to call Roy Wilkins."[‡] Not deterred, I said: "Call the students. I'm the only one sitting here with these people who can speak for those people back there in Cambridge, so call them." I remember James Forman, every time we'd try to get hold of him, he was at a different airport. I knew that was a lie. They'd come back: "Well, his office says he's not there. He's on his way to something—maybe at the airport."

The young people came back to the Movement by that summer. They had gotten kind of defeated. Donna, my oldest daughter, doesn't remember that, but they did. But then once it got going again, they came back—and brought others. There was one huge day when we had three or four generations of people in jail out of families in the town, grandmothers and mothers and kids. That's the night the mayor called for the National Guard because they had arrested us for sitting in restaurants. Then the kids came out, and the police were abusing them. We used to have spotters out, and they went back and told the black community. And then by twelve at night, you could hear the roar.

---

[*]The CIG, a nonviolent group, walked from Baltimore to Washington, D.C., to protest discrimination and staged demonstrations and other activities. Mrs. Richardson supported student activists and received their support.

[‡]NAACP leader and moderate.

Those of us in jail thought, "What on earth is that?" But it was just the whole community coming out, some people in nightgowns and everything. I understand if they had guns and knives and stuff, they left it in the courthouse lawn the next day. There were so many people that Cambridge had to call around to other places on the Shore, to Easton and Salisbury, to see if they would take them. And their jailsmen said no.

At one point, we were in jail, and I refused to come out, because they sent for the Maryland State Interracial Committee and they were meeting, but nobody had said anything about our five demand areas. A lot of the people took bail because the jail was overcrowded, but some of us stayed in. It was during that period of eight or nine days that Judge Laird Henry tried to set up a committee of the influential people who controlled the town to try to get some of our demands. And of course, the business people in town just wouldn't have it.

In the courtroom, the judge gave me a personal lecture: "How could you do your grandfather that way? He was this. He was that. You didn't come up that way. Why you acting like this?" He sentenced us to pay a one-penny fine. He had some relationship with my grandfather. There was some relationship between my grandfather and the other side of town, but I don't know what that was. But I do know that their family came to all the funerals. Cambridge had a very strange history.

The next thing, of course, was the National Guard. I think otherwise we may have been dead by now, but Gelston, the commander of the Guard, was fair. I think he had been there two weeks, and some of the sheriff's people had beat somebody black in the jail. So he took all the sheriff's people out and put his people in the jail. The black community was very pleased with that. He did what he had to do as far as being general of the National Guard and preventing this and that. But he wasn't mean. He wasn't.

White folks started spitting on the Guard and calling them kikes and chinks and stuff. He wouldn't say the guards were nonracist, but it saved them. They weren't gonna be on the side of white Cambridge, anyhow. And, of course, the elderly women in the black community—for a while this really annoyed me—were going out in the hot summertime with ice tea and lemonade and cookies and giving them to the guard on the corner. Which I really was not pleased with. I remember one child, Derrick Cephas, I don't know how the guard found out that he was extremely bright, but they had a National Guard uniform tailored for him, and he used to stand on the corner with them. Oh! I used to want to slap him! But, anyhow, it worked out.

The other thing is, it was a whole different structure. As soon as that National Guard came in, eight o'clock, nobody was out, black or white; businesses shut down; no alcohol was sold. My cousin came to see me from Pennsylvania, and I didn't even really know because I'd never dealt with a curfew, but they had shut down the roadway, the entrance into Cambridge. It was a total shutdown at the time. Then they ended up saying people had to get back and forth on the buses. I know it had to do with business—maids, I bet.

The press, after they'd been in there for three or four weeks, began to understand. Those guys had to stay there, and stay in the motels and stuff. I think after the first few months, we got surprisingly good coverage for that time. And the *Times* had a lot of articles.

All I remember is they wanted to shut Cambridge down just like they wanted to shut Ferguson down. And it wasn't shut down. So during that period of time, everybody—state, federal—had to talk. They had to deal with me. They couldn't insult you at that point, by the time they realized what was going on. Because the main thing is they wanted the people out of the streets.

The money was running on the National Guard. They had been there for eighteen months. It looked bad for the United States. The guys in the Guard were getting ready to lose their jobs, because they had to rotate them from each county every month, and businesses would give them thirty days. So our thing during that period of time was mainly to go out in the streets and make them come out and stop us, so they wouldn't leave town. So the government had to keep spending money.

The governor certainly didn't want to have the National Guard there out in the street for eighteen months. I think Robert Kennedy threatened everybody in the state of Maryland, including the governor. Because we weren't going to the polls and we weren't going to the politicians. There were no political people involved in Cambridge.

March on Washington

I think it was Courtland Cox that called to ask me to speak at the March on Washington, and I agreed.

They told me to please dress up, because by that time I was wearing jeans—well, they called them dungarees—and blouses, because you never knew when you were gonna be arrested and upended in the street. So I said, "All right." It was late. The march was maybe about ten days away. I was coordinating the people that wanted to go from the Eastern Shore. My original instinct was just like Malcolm X said, to go there and lay in the streets. I think a lot of people in SNCC thought that, but as you know, the Kennedys and people got in there and manipulated it into a nice picnic.

The people in my county and town wanted to go. So we had to coordinate that. When he said he wanted me to dress up, I didn't know what the hell that was about. So my mother and I went all over the Eastern Shore—we were boycotting in Cambridge—to find a jean skirt. They were not like they are today. We finally found this jean skirt with suspenders, and I got a white blouse, and I wore it.

On the day of the march, I was taken and put in a whole separate

.

white tent. There were no men there. Dorothy Height was there. I remember her hat. And some other women. I was wondering where Diane Nash was. I didn't know until after everything was over that she wasn't there.

Height came over to me and said, "We're going to the ladies' room and we'll be back." They had been late picking me up from the hotel, so I did not have to go to the bathroom. So I said, "Okay. I'll sit here and wait." There was a satellite news crew there from Europe, and the guy started interviewing me there, and then Bayard Rustin came up and said, "What are you doing here?" And I said, "What do you mean, what am I doing? I'm waiting for the women to come back." He said, "No. They up on the stage." So I thought, "What?" So then he takes me through the crowd and shows me where to go on the stage. But before we get there, I met Lena Horne with Rosa Parks, and she was putting her in front of the foreign news crews and saying, "This is the woman that started it."

So I thought, "Yeah, let me help her do this." So I went to another one of the TV installations with her. Then I ran into the SNCC people, who were upset because march leaders were trying to stop John Lewis's speech that Courtland Cox and Jim Forman had helped write. The SNCC people said, "Come go with us, because they wouldn't let us back in the Lincoln Monument. Maybe they'll let you in." I tried, but they wouldn't let me in either.

So, I came back, and when I went up on the stage, there was Josephine Baker. I had heard about her all my young life, so I was kind of overwhelmed. She said to me, "They took your chair." I said, "What chair?" Then I saw they had chairs, and they had banners across them with the women's names. So she said, "You need to raise hell." But I said, "No. I have more important things to do." Because I saw Robert Ming* from Chicago and I had some legal question I wanted to ask. So I went to the back of the whole stage.

---

*A lawyer with the NAACP Legal Defense Fund who served on the legal team for *Brown v. Board of Education*, among other cases.

At some point, they called our names, and then people said to me, "Well, go up there and say something." I have never been a fantastic charismatic speaker anyhow, so I went up there and I was going say, "Stay here until they pass that no-good civil rights bill." I said, "Hello," and the man snatched the microphone.

I don't know what it was; people said it was because I was a woman. I think it was because Cambridge was so toxic that they didn't want me anywhere near there. A friend of my godmother's who was an assistant attorney general at the Department of the Interior said they had meetings before that day saying that I was a whore, I would do anything to grandstand and make them mess up that day, and whatever. And he was trying to tell them, "You know, I was raised with her as a child."

I don't think it was because I was a woman, although I have to say that when we first started, one of the men on the committee said, "Anyway, we don't understand women, and so they won't know whether you're for real or not." And, as far as he was concerned, that was a good strategy, because they'd always be off-base. Anyhow, that was what went on that day at the march. I didn't think of what happened to me as sexist. I just thought that they felt threatened by Cambridge because they couldn't get us out of the streets.

The People Were Speaking Through Me

I don't know why I didn't back down from threats. I was afraid. But I think it must be like soldiers—you get in stuff and you fear, and then you go forward and you fear until it kind of . . . not settles in, but becomes part of you, and you don't necessarily recognize it as fear because you're constantly exposed to it.

The people I went to school with at Howard kept writing me from all over, saying, "You were so shy and retiring. How are you doing this?" I mean, they weren't necessarily disagreeing. But I was shy. I think at some point in that process, I felt that the people in the Second Ward moved toward me and spoke through me, and that allowed me to take action. Whatever else happened in my life, from those three years I had a sense of accomplishment.

I gained the confidence to lead inch by inch and day by day. I probably think about it more now, since people are going back and doing history, than I did then. Because I just considered myself a civil rights worker. And that's what we were doing. Of course, at that time, '63 or '64, in SNCC, I don't care what you were doing in the community, everybody appreciated everybody else. It wasn't like SCLC or NAACP—it wasn't that structure.

I don't know what happened to Occupy—I'm sure it was a lot of weight put on them—but I actually do think that unstructured works better. When you have a straight hierarchy, you have to have votes on this, and a crisis happens so you have to have a meeting, and everybody votes maybe a month later when the crisis is over and whatever the people think about it is disappearing. So I would stay unstructured.

We weren't in for a formalized, century-old organization where you would have to kind of shave your position and switch your position in order to get grants, or back off in order to get the money to pay your staff and host annual awards dinners. I mean, we weren't there to be permanent, because we didn't think civil rights was a business. We were pretty sure we were going to see some of the victories. I did not think I was gonna make a life career out of it if I lived.

Direct Action

I admire Fannie Lou Hamer, Rosa Parks, Diane Nash, Kathleen Cleaver. Mainly because we were activists. A lot of the others had organizations and stuff. I probably would have given you a different answer four or five years ago, but I think the Movement lost power when the government moved in and negotiated with SNCC to not do direct action, but to do voter registration. Now they're doing the same thing in Ferguson.

I think Diane Nash, myself, maybe a couple of others, were in for maintaining direct action. According to an old *Ramparts* article, they say they gave the men in SNCC deferments. So, what I thought was a philosophical argument about direct action and voter registration may have also had some other dynamics. That was through the National Student Association, which had the same acronym as the NSA now. *Ramparts* laid it out.*

There was a government push to push the Movement into voter registration. I guess that's why I was so furious the other day when people on the SNCC email list started saying, "Send people out to register to vote." What is this, 2014? Those people must have some reason for not voting. I mean, you don't go vote when people have their foot on your neck. You just let them have the foot on your neck.

Besides, the people in Cambridge in the Second Ward voted. There were five churches. Those church people went out and saw that they voted. You don't keep voting when it's not improving your condition. I saw where one of the Swarthmore students said that people didn't vote, but that wasn't true. In Cambridge it wasn't an issue. There would be no point in us doing voter registration. We've been voting since 1850.

---

*The article referenced is "NSA and the CIA" by Sol Stern, appearing in *Ramparts* magazine, March 1967, pp. 29–39. Included in the revelations about CIA funding for the National Student Association's international programs is the granting of draft deferments for NSA leaders, who were deemed to have an "occupation vital to the national interest." No connection to SNCC is put forward. Many sources suggest that male civil rights activists were targeted for induction in order to remove them from communities, rather than granted any form of protection from the draft.

I grew up in my grandfather's house. I know how politicians do. It doesn't matter whether you're Democrat or Republican. And that's true today in Congress, in the White House. I'm sure that those people that have the money and power in this country do not go and vote. You don't see any pictures of them out at the polls, I can't think of that. "Whoa, it's Bill Gates's vote. There's Bill Gates. He's going to vote." Or, "There's so and so." No. That's not to say they don't try to control things. But they don't wield control by voting.

Lessons for Activists

Activists have to be ready to give up a couple years of their life. I mean, that's one thing in SNCC: if they had just started college, they eventually gave up for a couple years and went back. I think you have to devote all your time to that. And I don't think you should accept it, but I don't think you need to think that praying and singing your way is going to get you out of trouble.

I don't have a religious background. I don't think preachers are gonna free us. I just think black folks think that they have to wait until they die and go to heaven and be happy. I mean, that's part of the theology. That's why on the plantation they picked the person that was going to be a preacher.

My mother used to say I was stubborn. But that's not any kind of philosophical position. I think it was because that ran through my family. Both my grandparents were what I guess they would call privileged now. They had money. But how did that make a difference in how I was treated in civic spaces?

You have to be listening to the people you're representing, being a spokesman for. Sometimes it may be slower than you expect, or maybe not. The people in Ferguson, hopefully there's a lot of them across the country. But in fact, the whole school thing across the country is segregated again. So, that's not because black folks didn't go out and vote.

Up here on the Upper West Side, they had one all-black high school and one white one, right on the liberal Upper West Side. That's crazy. I mean, I've been in New York all that time, and when I saw it, I thought: "God." I guess if somebody ordinary had walked in and told me that, I'd have thought, "Where on earth did they get that from?" Despite the fact that I knew that they didn't get rid of the residential segregation. And just the other day, some jerk said the government's never tried to implement the Fair Housing Act. So where have all these people been all these years? The fifty years they celebrated last August.

Cambridge Today

We go down to Cambridge every year. A guy I've known since he was a little boy in Cambridge said that he comes through there and this is gone and that's gone. But there is a black woman mayor, and the head of the city council is a black man. The blacks are on various civic and governmental committees and structures. Whether it has been successful beyond that, I don't know.

Now, one thing that did happen: in order to get the new housing, they had to take out the part of the charter that restricted blacks to the Second Ward. Of course, we also had to say, well, whites could come in too. A housing development was put in a space where whites could move if they wanted to. I think one or two did. Anyhow, they had to take that "only blacks live in this space" clause out of the charter. I don't know why it was first put in. But Cambridge, apparently, from the Bay Bridge down to Cambridge on both sides of the road, was a huge plantation of the Lloyds. So something went on there. I guess either they freed the slaves or they were already free, and they put them all in this little box.

Books Are Good

I don't know what they were doing in the South, but we had Negro history in school every year. We found whatever we could and made scrapbooks out of it, devoted to whatever was known, whatever's there.

I was at an event recently where I said to the organizer, "Well, I wonder." I said, "I have a great-grandchild. When he has social studies, I wonder what he gets." Because I had just seen a *New York Times Book Review* thing: there's no black books out there, no books with black people in them out there. She said to me, "No, no, no. Don't ask him because you'll get hysterical. I guarantee you'll get hysterical." So, when I saw him the next time, I asked him, "What do you have for social studies? You got any current events?" "Nope." I knew he wasn't gonna get quote-unquote "black stuff," but I thought maybe, and he said, "No."

I think some of the professionals should do something about that. They could write historical stuff. Books are good. They could oversee some students or write it themselves in a smaller, more compact way for teenagers or young readers. Or the graphic arts stuff. Of course, I haven't seen it, but when I asked about books on the Internet, someone said: "Oh, John Lewis has a graphic novel." But I didn't mean just John Lewis. We need more written about any of the areas where stuff was going on.

I Want Them to Get It Straight

Very few people have interviewed me. They're saying what they thought. I find, I guess, because I'm still here, that there's some changes—stuff that even, maybe years ago, was published in books or in narratives, and now it looks like they're set. I think they deliberately sanitize stuff.

I have no idea how I would want my obituary to read, except that if they write an article, I want them to get it straight. To say that I was able to become part of the people and carry their hopes and desires and internalize it and carry out into the public space and win some things.

Gloria Richardson speaks at the 2017 fiftieth anniversary celebration of the Cambridge Movement. (Photo courtesy of the *Dorchester Banner*, Cambridge, Maryland)

Myrlie Evers-Williams joined more than two thousand delegates to the NAACP convention in Washington in a pilgrimage to her late husband Medgar Evers's grave in Arlington National Cemetery on June 25, 1964. (Credit: Getty Images)

9

MYRLIE EVERS

Born Myrlie Beasley in Vicksburg, Mississippi, in 1933, she was raised by her aunt and grandmother. When she was seventeen and a student at Alcorn A&M College in Lorman, Mississippi, she met her future husband, Medgar Evers. They married when she was eighteen. She credits Medgar as influential in shaping her lifelong commitment to activism. Most Americans, watching her deliver the invocation at the second inauguration of President Barack Obama in 2013, would likely be surprised to know of her heroic history.

When Medgar Evers was appointed the first NAACP field secretary in the state of Mississippi in 1954, he negotiated a paid position for Myrlie as the office's secretary. A Mississippi native, she knew the dangers of activism for racial equality and understood how her husband's prominence would bring unwanted attention and pressure to their lives. Their home was firebombed in 1962. In June 1963, Medgar Evers was assassinated in their driveway. Then a widow with three small children, Myrlie Evers stayed in their home in Mississippi for a year after the assassination of her husband, where the driveway was an emotionally intense daily reminder of her husband's death. In the summer of 1964, she addressed the NAACP convention at the time when civil rights workers James Chaney, Andrew Goodman, and Michael Schwerner were missing and not yet discovered murdered.

She and her husband had often talked about California as a possible place to move someday, so she decided to take their children there. At the age of thirty-one, she went back to college, working part time, and graduated from Pomona College in 1968 with a degree in sociology.

After Medgar's death, Evers was the sole provider for her family. Hardworking, she was the director for community affairs for the Atlantic Richfield Company during the 1970s, a position that allowed her to support her family. Even while working in the corporate sector, Evers maintained her commitment to civil rights and public service, waging an unsuccessful campaign for a seat in the U.S. House of Representatives in the 1970s, then becoming the first black woman to serve on the Los Angeles Board of Public Works in 1987. At age sixty-two in 1995, Evers ran for and won a hard-fought election as the chair of the NAACP, serving in that position until 1998 and helping to reinvigorate the organization, which had been beset by financial and structural problems.

Evers vigilantly pursued justice for the murder of her husband, a three-decade commitment that ended when the killer, whose early trials had resulted in hung juries, was convicted in 1994. The killer, avowed white supremacist Byron de la Beckwith, was well known in the Jackson area. De la Beckwith openly flaunted his hatred for blacks and his contempt for the legal system.

The Evers home is now a museum, given by the family to Tougaloo College. It received a national landmark dedication in 2017. The home is on a quiet, unassuming residential street, bringing into sharp focus the terror that was a part of the everyday lives of African American leaders during the Civil Rights Movement.

NAACP Legal Defense and Educational Fund lawyer Derrick Bell stayed in the Evers home a week prior to the assassination of Medgar Evers. He was the attorney for the older Evers son in a suit to desegregate the Jackson schools. Derrick slept in the living room with volunteer armed guards. African American residents knew that while the Movement was nonviolent in philosophy and practice, others were not; black people also believed in self-defense.

Myrlie Evers has kept faith with the Movement ideals and strug-gles while forging an extraordinary life for herself and her children.

She remains beautiful, gracious, grateful, and propelled by an invisible life force—a mixture of compassion, curiosity, and righteous anger. Her candor and openness can shock one expecting to encoun-ter a martyr or saint. She is defiantly a whole person. For African Americans, preserving personhood is itself an accomplishment.

In the interview, Evers reflects on her leadership, her working partnership with her husband, both professional and domestic, as well as her own activism for gender equality, her triumph over grief and anger, and her fight to reinvigorate the NAACP.

Challenging the System

I was seventeen years old when I met Medgar. Eighteen years old when I married him.

Trouble was, when I met Medgar, I was told that I should not reach for the stars. I should reach for the moon and beyond that, and it was all right to challenge the system, which was unfair to us. So, my introduction to what you would call the Civil Rights Movement actually started with him helping this young, untrained eye and mind to look at the future, and to be willing to work and to sacrifice so that my people, in particular—people of color, generally—would have the same opportunities that everyone else in America would have.

I came from a family of teachers. People who try to have the best life that they could provide for us children. Civil rights was not a part of that. You want to achieve the highest standards that you could reach without shaking the system at all. I was very fortunate to be surrounded by people who loved me dearly. My grandmother and my aunt who reared me told me I could accomplish anything that I set my mind to do as long as I stayed within the boundaries of what society had set for me.

Medgar came along and said, "You can do whatever you want to do, but keep those boundaries out of the way. If you're reaching for the stars and the moon is higher, you reach for the moon. And if there's something else higher than that, you reach for that." You never stop climbing. You never stop dreaming for something higher and better.

Medgar was a veteran of World War II, as was my father. When Medgar returned to Mississippi, he decided to confront the rampant prejudice and racism. I came along and learned as we moved forward in the work—in the Mississippi Delta, and then later in Jackson, Mississippi.

That was my initiation into the Civil Rights Movement.

Woman's Role in Our Society Behind
the Cotton Curtain

Medgar and I moved to the Mississippi Delta, a town called Mound
Bayou. It is a historic little place because it was formed by former
slaves. I'm not sure about this, but I think it was the only town of
that kind in Mississippi, certainly of that size, and it was small. It
was there where Medgar worked. Both of us worked for the Mag-
nolia Mutual Life Insurance Company, very southern. Medgar took
it upon himself to go to the plantations around that area and sell
insurance to the sharecroppers. That was brave on his part, because
he was looked at with quite a bit of suspicion.

Fast forward. Medgar was the first known African American
to apply for admission to the University of Mississippi, Ole Miss.
He applied to the law school. We were still living in Mound Bayou
at that time. He went to visit with Dr. E. J. Stringer, president of
the NAACP Mississippi State Conference, who I believe lived in
Columbus, Mississippi, to talk about the NAACP supporting him
in a suit. He was going to file a suit for admittance. Instead, they
talked him into taking the position as the first field secretary for the
NAACP and opening an office in Jackson, Mississippi. An office on,
now historic, Farish Street in Jackson, Mississippi, and later in the
Masonic Temple building near Jackson State University. That's how
we came to be in Jackson.

A very, very interesting time. I was a very good typist, IBM punch
card operator, all of those things that elevated the woman's role in
our little society at that time. I did practically everything that had to
be done in that office. It was not only organizing events, or celebra-
tions, or even the sad things to acknowledge people who had been
hurt, who had been killed. I did research for his speeches. I even
wrote some of his speeches.

We were behind the cotton curtain, if you will. Not the iron curtain, the cotton curtain, because you could not get information out

to the wire services that you could in any other part of the country. It meant being concise with what you reported and sending that information to the NAACP office in New York City, and you did it by telegram.

So I researched; I wrote. I was a welcoming committee to people who came in. I found myself in the role of being hostess with the mostest, but the mostest was nothing because we really had nothing to give but heartfelt personality and welcoming. I was his support system. Interestingly enough, we had an understanding that once we entered into that office, I became Mrs. Evers and he became Mr. Evers. We kept it very formal, kept all outside things outside.

I was very afraid because I knew what we were doing was different. Medgar had made number one on the death list in Mississippi. I come from a family of teachers, and really not accustomed to being a, if you will, "troublemaker." I had to adapt to all of that along with rearing, at that time, two children.

I became a jack-of-all-trades. I did everything. I did research. I did the writing. I did the printing. I did everything that one would do as a secretary and I had the role of being hostess. I also had the responsibilities, of course, of our children. I found it, at times, overwhelming, because I asked the question that I think women, certainly, began to ask: "What about me? Where am I in all of this?" And there was the fear that one day I might lose my husband and my children as well as myself. I could be maimed or something.

From time to time people did come visit and it was a little difficult to actually house people because our house was so small, but we always found a place, in a way, to do that. I think of Thurgood Marshall. I think of others like Constance Baker Motley. I think of Attorney Bell. Everyone visited our house. I think I fail to mention that I was a cook and bottle washer as well. I did it all. I'm reflecting back now to this refrigerator that we had that had a freezer section about as wide as this and as deep as this. It would get so little. And what a terrible time I had trying to balance a budget of twenty-five dollars every two weeks feeding and housing people coming in and all, but it was our home.

Now, it was also a hub. It was a place people came where they felt safe, where they could talk. Even our few Caucasian friends would come to our house as well, but they would park a block or so away and walk so that their cars would not be noted. Because the police would drive by every so often and take down tag numbers. It was an active, passionate time with fear lurking right around the corner. In a sense, I think, fear made it even more exciting. Perhaps exciting is the wrong word to use, but you felt more dutiful as a group. It was similar to an underground railroad type of operation.

We bonded, and there are still a few of us that are still around. To be able to reach out and touch, and say we have been there. That was something that particularly happened a couple of months ago with the fiftieth anniversary of Medgar's assassination. You never lose the passion. You lose the fear because that's something you have to overcome to be able to move forward, but it's a time of remembrance, a time of thankfulness. And I can't tell you how blessed I feel to have lived a large part of my life during that time.

It was an exciting but frightening time, because you stared at death every day, and you walked and death walked along with you. But there was always hope, and there were always people who surrounded you to give you a sense of purpose. That they needed you in many different ways, and as in the song that we sang so much, one day, we shall overcome. So, for a very, very young sheltered wife, there were the thrills, but there was the pain, and there was the fear that I believe at that time probably took over my life.

You're So Much Stronger Than You Think You Are

You try to prepare. You do a little role playing. I personally would put myself in a position mentally where I had just lost my husband.

I knew it was coming. I knew it was coming. What do you do? How do you conduct your life? How do you take care of your children? It may seem a little sick, but you try as best you can to prepare yourself for the moment when it all becomes a reality, because you know it's going to.

I recall a conversation with Medgar not too long before his assassination. I said to him, "I can't live without you. I can't make it without you." And he looked at me and said, "You're much stronger than you think you are. You're so much stronger than you think you are. You will be okay. You must believe it."

I had such faith and confidence in him. He was my hero as well as my husband and father of my children. He instilled in me a belief that I too could rise to whatever occasion was presented and be successful in dealing with it, in moving forward. We spoke, not that often, but we did speak to the fact of location. Where would we move if we ever left Mississippi? Of course, he said, "I know I'm going to die, and wherever I'm going, to heaven or hell, I'm going from Mississippi." And he truly believed all that. I did not always want to live here. I really didn't.

Born, bred, educated in Mississippi, but Mississippi was not a love of mine. It was not a passion as it was for Medgar. I knew that I had to find a peaceful place for my children. Good schools and a place where we could recover as best as we could. After his demise, I knew that I had to go back to school. I had two years of college and dropped out a semester after we got married. I had children. My family was still in Mississippi, but Medgar had said, "If we ever leave this state, we're going to California." After his death during that time, everything I did was based on what I thought he would have wanted.

In that first year, I remained in Jackson, Mississippi, with my children. The NAACP promoted me—I was about to use the word "used," that's more accurate—but promoted me as the widow. And quite honestly, I was a fundraising instrument for the NAACP.

That's something I hope to write about in the future because it needs to be said. I think of myself. I think of Fannie Lou Hamer, and I think of a couple of other women—Emmett Till's mother, Mamie Till—who were really used to rally support. Which is good. But also to raise a tremendous amount of money for the cause. And I don't think either of us received any compensation for that at all. That's another story of the Movement.

I would leave my children on the weekends and go wherever I was asked to go. I would speak. The audiences were always responsive. I watched people open their purses or pull their wallets out of their pants and literally empty money into our containers. We never saw any of the money at all. But that was part of the Movement then. I don't think that would happen today, because most people are sophisticated enough to say, "No, I will not be used. If you're going to do this, then I have a percentage that I will get out of that." But that's what happened during that time.

Today when I visit my former home, which my children and I deeded to Tougaloo College as a museum, I can still see the blood. We needed to get away from that place. Our oldest son, Darrell Kenyatta, reached a point where he refused to eat, he would not study, he would not talk. He went into this very, very angry withdrawal mode. I knew we needed to be away from the house. My daughter would go to bed with her dad's picture, holding it every night. The youngest one, Van, who was three, would go to bed with this little rifle. I knew that we could no longer live in that house.

I was told in my family that to hate someone was a sin. I bucked all of that. I was so angry. I was so filled with hatred. I survived in the middle of the night dreaming of what I would do to extract my pound of flesh from all of those who had done wrong to my family, to my husband. So, I have a split personality. People would tell me, "Oh, you are so strong. You are so good. You are so forgiving." Well, I would smile and say, "Thank you."

And inside? I was boiling. At night, I fantasized about what I would do. I even reached the point—and this was not a fantasy—in the first few months after Medgar's death, I called a man in our particular neighborhood where we lived. I called him, I said, "I need you to do something for me. We know who pulled the trigger. Find him and bring him to me." I remember how shocked they were. "You don't mean that." I said, "Yes, I do. Find him and bring him to me. Secure him and you leave. I'll take care of the rest."

So, in a sense, there I was with this split personality: the grieving yet understanding strong widow, and a person who wanted vengeance like I needed water. A woman who was lonely and afraid, but one who was determined to make it. And somewhere in all of that, I decided that the best thing I could do to make society pay for the loss of my husband was to be successful in whatever it was that I decided to do. So, that was the turn in my life.

Everything that I did was based on what I thought Medgar would have wanted, and the promises that I made to him the night before he was killed. California seemed to be the only place. I wanted to go back to school. So I went on this venture a year or so after Medgar's assassination and relocated. As my grandmother said to me, "You run as far away from Mississippi as you could get without going into the ocean." Claremont, California, became home for us, but it was a struggle. The children had an easier time. I think children adjust a little easier than adults even though they carry the nightmare with them. But California became home, and until this day it still is.

Women in the Movement

I think about women in the Movement. Recently, attending the fiftieth anniversary of the March on Washington, I remembered the struggle that women had, and how hard they fought to be a part of that program. To be recognized. We were still being pushed back. Not only by society, but by our own male counterparts.

Had it not been for Dorothy Height, I'm not sure that a woman would have been on that scheduled program of speakers at all, or that the march would have been what it was. But we don't get credit for everything that we do. She was the mother. She told the men, "Stop fighting amongst yourselves. Martin Luther King will speak on that program." Because there was an effort to keep him from being on that program. They put him at the end of the program thinking that everyone would be tired and walk away. But it turned out to be a singular moment in the life of the Movement and Dr. King.

Marian Wright Edelman was a very, very good role model. A brave young woman who came to Mississippi and worked almost without fear. I was incensed when she was unable to speak at the second March on Washington because the time had been usurped by someone else and there was not enough time for her to speak. She smiled and went on her way, and said, "I'm on to the next thing." She's a shining example of the kind of women that I think and would hope that most young women would want to emulate. I can think of others along the way who have just done so much such as Marian, but I'm not so sure how many people remember or know of the work that she and other women did in Mississippi. They should.

I think of Fannie Lou Hamer. "I'm sick and tired of being sick and tired." She and I attended a meeting, the organizing meeting of the National Women's Political Caucus in Washington, D.C., in 1971. We came together, some three hundred of us, and we discussed the kind of women we did not want and the kind of woman that needed to be brought in politics. And we were debating whether we should support male candidates with funds or should it be for women only. People would get up and go to the microphone and talk: pro/con. Fannie Lou Hamer walks up to the microphone and she says, "I'm here because I'm strong." Yes, you are. "There's not a man who ever did anything for me. I'm here on my own strength."

That time, I couldn't take it anymore. I was standing in line, and when my time came, I said, "What about the men who feel the same way we do about certain subjects, should we neglect them? We should include them. We should be inclusive." I turned and I said to her, wherever she was sitting, "Fannie Lou Hamer, you don't speak the truth." You could hear the silence in that auditorium. I said, "If it had not been for Medgar Evers who supported you, who helped you, you would not be where you are today." And I turned around, sat down. Three years passed before she spoke to me again. Every time I saw her, I would delight in speaking to her because I knew it would make her so angry.

We finally reached the point where she said to me, "I understand where you were coming from, and you were right." And I said, "Yes, I know I was right. I'm a woman. We are not treated fairly in American society, certainly not in politics." I had run for two offices, then. I said, "But we cannot afford to neglect those, the males, who support us." "Oh, yeah," she said. And I said, "Oh, yeah." And we embraced, and that was the end of that.

I Stand on My Own as a Woman

I want to share this one thing with you. I am presently observing a change within the organization I worked with for so long, and Medgar worked and gave his life for: the NAACP. More women are on the board holding important positions. The soon-to-be executive is a woman. The chairman of the board is a woman. I say that because when I was elected chairman of the board of the NAACP, there were only fourteen women on that sixty-four-member board.

I was told, "You can't do this job, move out of the way. You are only Medgar's widow." Oh, yes. And I recall my response. Not very ladylike. I said, "Get the hell out of my way." Because I was determined to do what I could to help turn that organization around. My first year as chairman of the board was a year in hell because the men did not want to give up one ounce of the control that they had. We had board meetings that lasted far too long, where there was so much anger, so much to be done about the organization itself.

At this one particular board meeting, which lasted about six or seven hours, I held the gavel the entire time. A couple of men came up to me, and they said, "Tell me, why did you never turn that gavel over to the other person, Chairman?" And I said, "Because had I done that, the entire agenda that we went through, the problems that we solved, would have been undone while I was in the restroom." They laughed. "Well, how on earth did you not go?" I said, "Evidently, you've never run for political office. Because if you had, you would know that you don't drink anything, not even a sip of water, during that time so you can stand firm with that gavel in your hand." You know what they told me? They brought another couple of powerful men who said, "You won us over." I said, "Where is the bathroom?" And they laughed, but I was treated like something to be kicked aside all that time. That's my book.

Women have had such a struggle. I have been identified more as Medgar's widow than any of the other things that I have done. And there have been occasions when I have had to say, "I'm more than just a widow. I'm my own woman." I have carved out my own path with the help of others, but I stand on my own as a woman. As my husband told me, "You're strong. You're bright. You can do whatever you want to do."

I still hold that near and dear now, and I think about the young women today. Many of them who could care less about the women who paved the way for the doors that are open now. Some of them think that they've done it all by themselves, and that's the group that I would like to just bring in and say, "Sit. Read. Listen. Learn. You didn't do it by yourselves. There were others who paved the way with blood, sweat, and tears." The grammar might not have been correct, no. They might have sung out of tune. They may have not dressed well. They might have been overweight. They might not have known the latest dances. But they had that good old common sense and joy in the heart to move us forward.

I said to a group of young men in corporate America, "You know you're fighting us." "Why do you think we're fighting you?" I said, "This competition between us, I'm not sure either of us are winning at this point." And I said, "No, you all thought you have it, but you didn't. Because corporate America was playing one against the other, and you are still locked into that momma syndrome." "Well, what's that?" "Momma was the one, in slavery, who always had some little job. She took care of her family. That's momma. And today, what do you do? You look at the pretty ones and you say, 'Hey, hot momma.'" So, there's a savior and there's a sex object, and somewhere you have to kind of meld those two together and not let society part us. Fighting over the crumbs that are there. We have to make the pie. We have to make the cake. We have to make the bread. And we have to work together.

It's very interesting to me to see where we have come in this last fifty years. I mean everybody, but women in particular, because we're still dealing with challenges that we should not have to, but we're rising to those challenges. Just don't forget those of us who struggled to get us this far. That's my wish. My hope.

I visited an exhibit on Medgar here in Jackson at the Department of Archives and History. Impressive. Small, but impressive. There was an anteroom off to the side. I asked, "Oh, what's that?" They said, "Well, it's a little personal. You may not want to see it." And I said, "Is it about Medgar?" "Yes." I said, "Of course I want to see it." I walked in the room and there was the rifle that was used to kill him, in Plexiglas. And I was stunned. I felt this hot flash just go through my body, and I looked at the rifle, and I guess it was a vision of sorts. The butt part with the trigger said, "Hatred." The part forward, I could literally see Medgar's body faced down, dying or dead. And just above him, coming out of that rifle was the fire.

And it said to me, "He knew what his job was, and he did it." He knew the price that he would have to pay. He still stepped up and did it. He is free, and there's hope for everyone else in that fire. That was just a few weeks ago. And it's marvelous that I had this vision because it helped to free me from that remaining hatred that I had in my heart and in my soul.

After all of these years of all the anger, the hurt, the fear, I finally know the anger was a blessing because it saved me. It gave me a purpose for living. To prove that you took my husband, but you did not take his memories. You did not take our love. Look, there's three children. Our eldest son, Darrell Kenyatta, filed a suit in his name to open up the school system in Mississippi. When I think of our children and what they went through, and see where they are and what they have done, it's okay.

Out of the anger, out of the hatred, came a very strong woman. I'll say that about myself. A very strong woman who did well academically, who did well in business in corporate America, who did well in politics even though it was a time when very few women were running. I did. I didn't win, but it helped to change areas where I ran. And I can go on with a number of things that, ordinarily, I would have thought, "I can't do that." But I stepped out and I did it when women were still struggling trying to say to the world, "Look, here we are. We have something to give, something to contribute. Let us in."

When these areas would not allow us in the door we stepped out and built our own businesses, and gave ourselves a title. A president, a CEO. We developed all kinds of wonderful volunteer positions to help heal the wounded soul, the sick, the feeble. It's been a turning point, all for women. And regardless of how bad things are, we can always take it and turn it around to something positive if we dare do so.

So, here I am today tired. Tired, but so thankful for everything that happened. How many of us have an opportunity to know what it is we want to do and feel so strongly about it that we give our all to that cause?

Doubly Blessed

But you know? You don't stop living. Years and years later, I met a man who became my second husband, Walter Williams. I was doubly blessed because we were very, very good friends for the longest time. He told me that he had seen my children and I on television being interviewed by Dan Rather, and he said, "What's in your backyard?" He looked at that interview and said, "God, I wanna take care of that man's family." I teased him about it. I said, "Be careful what you ask for. You might get it."

Well, we were very, very good friends. I met him years after I moved to California. I was so fortunate to be able to have another opportunity at joy and happiness. It was not the passionate first love that I had with Medgar, but it was a good solid friendship, respect type of thing. Walter was known as the person who sued the Longshoremen's Union for jobs. So he knew all of the pain, and people trying to beat you and shooting at you and whatnot, and was such a strong admirer of Medgar's. My children loved Pops. That's what they called him.

When some in the NAACP asked me to run for the chairmanship, I said, "No, I can't because I'm the caregiver for Walter." He was dying of prostate cancer. He told me, "This is the last thing I will ask you to do for me. You run and you win." I said yes. The day that I left to go to New York to the annual meeting, we embraced, and I told him, "Don't you go anywhere until I get back." And he said, "I'll try. I'll try." During those few days that I was in New York calling back and forth and talking to the hospice representatives and whatnot, they said, "Make your time short."

I waited until the day after my election and I called home, and at that point, he couldn't talk. I said, "I'm on my way." That plane could not move fast enough for me to get home to this man who was my friend, who admired Medgar, who had been so good to my children, Pops. When I finally got there, he couldn't talk, but he could motion with his eyes. And he lifted his feeble hand and tried to make a fist because I had won and he knew that. I got in bed with him, and I held him. Walter got what he wanted. He said he wanted to die at home in his bed with me next to him singing to him. And that's exactly what happened. I'm so thankful that I was able to do that.

People ask me about the name. Well, are you Evers-Williams? Or Evers? I say, "Both." I keep Evers because of my love and respect for my hero. I don't want the public to ever forget that man. There will be a time, and maybe it's coming up now, where I will write about Walter, and the work that he did, and the Longshoremen's Union, and breaking down barriers there, and the kind of relationship that we had. So, I sit here twice blessed. I sit here saying that women have such endurance. I sit here saying that we see far beyond what an ordinary view of life would be, and we never give up on living, and we never give up on positive change. And that's a part of the responsibility that all of us have. So, it's like, go for it.

A Lot Left in Me to Do

My next phase is survival. Survival in the sense of deciding what it is that I want to do. I'm eighty years of age. I have a feeling that there's still a lot left in me to do and to give. I'm a little tired. I would love to have a little rest, but there's something in me that says, "Not yet." So, once again, I'm searching to find what it is that's calling me. Because something is calling me.

I was not cut out to sit and twiddle my thumbs. I want to be active. I love working with young people. There's such a need to have African American young men brought into their own. I don't know how much of a role, but women could, should play in that. But on the other side, there are the young African American girls, and young women, and older women who think they've already made it, and who think they did it all by themselves. I'd like to embrace them with very strong arms, almost in crush, and say, "You still have so much to learn. Stop a moment. Read. Listen. Be directed. Don't forget those things and the people of the past that helped to get you to this point and into the future."

So I don't know what I'm going to do. Just stay busy and available for whatever comes my way, and I pray that I'll have the strength and the wisdom to do whatever shows its way to me.

I would hope that I would be remembered as a strong, honest, deeply committed to humankind type of woman who also believes in the need to have a little fun. Not to take one's self so seriously, to be open to new things, to be adventurous. I never thought in my wildest dreams that I would be asked by the president of the United States to deliver the prayer before his inauguration, as President Obama asked me to do. Dream big. Work hard. Work smart. And for me, I have to have my strong religious beliefs because, quite honestly, that's the only thing that has carried me through. In my deepest moments, there's a faith and there's trust. There's belief. There are possibilities.

Myrlie Evers-Williams listens to a dramatic reading as part of the
International Day of Remembrance Celebration honoring her late husband,
civil rights leader Medgar Evers on June 12, 2013, in Jackson, Mississippi, the
fiftieth anniversary of Evers's assassination. (Credit: AP Photo / Rogelio V.
Solis)

ACKNOWLEDGMENTS

Social justice advocacy and sharing the history of African Americans are lifelong passions of mine. Fortuitously, New Press executive editor Diane Wachtell shares similar passions and a publisher's zeal for presenting good stories. She brought me to The New Press—for which I will always be grateful. I thank my editor, Julie Enszer, for her dedicated and sensitive work on this book. She helped bring clarity, develop a compelling narrative, and bring forth a powerful book. I am grateful to the entire New Press team, all of whom have embraced this work. It is a distinct honor to be awarded the Ida and Studs Terkel Prize, which I accept in the memory of my beloved husband, Derrick Bell, and my beloved mother, Willie Mae Neal, to whom this book is dedicated.

Lighting the Fires of Freedom took root in my Antioch University Leadership and Change doctoral studies with my dissertation committee chaired by Dr. Alan E. Guskin, with committee members Dr. Laurien Alexandre, Dr. Elaine Gale, and Dr. Joseph Jordan. Outside mentor Dr. Beverly Guy-Sheftall helped illuminate the richness of African American women's history. Faculty librarian Deborah Baldwin was always on the case and on my side. My Antioch Sunday night study group, each of whom earned their doctorates before I did, held me in their hearts and across the finish line. They are family for life: Doctors Norman Dale, Naomi Nightingale, and Camilla Grace Fusae Ka'iuhono'onālani Wengler Vignoe.

Other Antioch faculty include the late Dr. Richard Couto. Dick Couto helped me find the courage to pursue my own vision of leadership and tell my story with authenticity and passion. The late Dr. Carolyn Kenny's humanity and sprit buoyed mine.

While railing against computer gremlins who were foiling my

formatting and slowing down the progress of my writing, I cried out to a writer friend, Betty Medsger, to see if she knew someone who could help me. What resulted was the beginning of a remarkable association with Ben Firestone, who, after a week or so of helping me meet formatting challenges, quietly mentioned that he was really an editor. I couldn't believe my good fortune. Ben's keen eye and gentle nature not only helped me complete my dissertation, he was my thought partner and writing and research associate as I began to turn the academic work into a book.

A chance encounter with Taj A. Brown at the 2017 Medgar Evers College commencement resulted in another very special business and literary association. With a background in the NAACP and the Children's Defense Fund, Taj's commitment to social justice and African American history mirror mine. His dedicated work and enthusiasm for this book helped in its completion.

Special thanks to three videographers, who captured several of my interviews on tape—George Griswold (Leah Chase and Myrlie Evers), Michael Johnson (Aileen Hernandez), and Tracey Heather Strain (Judy Richardson). Karen Chilton, a fine author in her own right, helped secure photographs and permissions for this book—no easy task, but one she accepted as a labor of love.

Dr. Kitty M. Steel has been my supporter and a role model for my entire doctoral journey. A lifelong learner, she earned her doctorate in her sixties as did I—and my first inspiration, the legendary scholar Dr. Anna Julia Cooper, who earned her doctorate at the age of sixty-four, becoming only the fourth African American woman to earn her doctorate.

The journey has been long, so there are many people to thank. I acknowledge daughters Lisa Marie Boykin, Lisa Jones, and Linda Singer, son Carter Robeson Bell, "little sis" Kaoula Harris, my brother Richard Neal, my late brothers Dr. William V. McCoy and David Neal, my godson Arthur Lee Butler, my goddaughter Lydia Stover, my nephew Christopher Eubanks, and cultural son Camilo

A. Romero. Others include Edith Benson, Madeleine Moore Burrell and Tom Burrell, Julie Burton of the Women's Media Center, Valerie Cavanaugh and William Kerstetter, Catherine Chadwick, Steve Clarke, Anne Cohen, Sheryl Cowan, Jonathan Delson, the late Ivanhoe Donaldson, Hazel N. Dukes, Reena Evers, Dr. Christina Greer, the late Lawrence Hamilton, Wilma Hayes, Roger Hickey, Jacob Holguin, Eleni Delimpaltadaki Janis, Sarah Johnson, Joe Lohwasser, Eddie Lopez, Dr. Marcella Maxwell, Mark Munger and Kate Bourne, Jessye Norman, Pamela and Charles Ogletree, MaryKay Penn, the late Raymond Petrie, Letty Cottin Pogrebin and Bertrand Pogrebin, Lindbergh Porter, Miles Rapoport, Stella Reese, Kenneth L. Roberson, the late Paulette Jones Robinson, Rashad Robinson, Markous Samaan, John Sexton, Rev. Dr. Paul Smith and Fran Smith, Cecile and Eric Springer, Lewis Steel, Gloria Steinem, Clyde Tate, Juhu Thukral, Lola C. West, and Sheng-Fu Yang.

The interviews with nine remarkable women are the heart and soul of this book. They are Leah Chase, Dr. June Jackson Christmas, Kathleen Cleaver, Myrlie Evers, Aileen Hernandez, Gay McDougall, Diane Nash, Gloria Richardson (Dandridge), and Judy Richardson. I thank them for their time, insights, and trust in sharing their stories. They made the road by walking and have devoted their lives to leading change. We are all in their debt.

INDEX

ABOUT THE AUTHOR

Janet Dewart Bell is a social justice activist with a doctorate in leadership and change from Antioch University. She founded the Derrick Bell Lecture on Race in American Society series at the New York University School of Law. An award-winning television and radio producer, she lives in New York City.

PUBLISHING IN THE PUBLIC INTEREST

Thank you for reading this book published by The New Press. The New Press is a nonprofit, public interest publisher. New Press books and authors play a crucial role in sparking conversations about the key political and social issues of our day.

We hope you enjoyed this book and that you will stay in touch with The New Press. Here are a few ways to stay up to date with our books, events, and the issues we cover:

- Sign up at www.thenewpress.com/subscribe to receive updates on New Press authors and issues and to be notified about local events
- Like us on Facebook: www.facebook.com/newpressbooks
- Follow us on Twitter: www.twitter.com/thenewpress

Please consider buying New Press books for yourself; for friends and family; or to donate to schools, libraries, community centers, prison libraries, and other organizations involved with the issues our authors write about.

The New Press is a 501(c)(3) nonprofit organization. You can also support our work with a tax-deductible gift by visiting www.thenewpress.com/donate.

THE STUDS AND
IDA TERKEL AWARD

On the occasion of his ninetieth birthday, Studs Terkel and his son, Dan, announced the creation of the Studs and Ida Terkel Author Fund. The Fund is devoted to supporting the work of promising authors in a range of fields who share Studs's fascination with the many dimensions of everyday life in America and who, like Studs, are committed to exploring aspects of America that are not adequately represented by the mainstream media. The Terkel Fund furnishes authors with the vital support they need to conduct their research and writing, providing a new generation of writers the freedom to experiment and innovate in the spirit of Studs's own work.

Studs and Ida Terkel Award Winners

David Dayen, *Chain of Title: How Three Ordinary Americans Uncovered Wall Street's Great Foreclosure Fraud*

Aaron Swartz, *The Boy Who Could Change the World: The Writings of Aaron Swartz* (awarded posthumously)

Beth Zasloff and Joshua Steckel, *Hold Fast to Dreams: A College Guidance Counselor, His Students, and the Vision of a Life Beyond Poverty*

Barbara J. Miner, *Lessons from the Heartland: A Turbulent Half-Century of Public Education in an Iconic American City*

Lynn Powell, *Framing Innocence: A Mother's Photographs, a Prosecutor's Zeal, and a Small Town's Response*

Lauri Lebo, *The Devil in Dover: An Insider's Story of Dogma v. Darwin in Small-Town America*